D0108375

MEN

MEN

notes from an
ongoing
investigation

LAURA KIPNIS

Metropolitan Books
Henry Holt and Company   New York

Metropolitan Books
Henry Holt and Company, LLC
Publishers since 1866
175 Fifth Avenue
New York, New York 10010
www.henryholt.com

Metropolitan Books® and ⊞® are registered trademarks of
Henry Holt and Company, LLC.

Library of Congress Cataloging-in-Publication data
Kipnis, Laura.
  Men : notes from an ongoing investigation / Laura Kipnis.—First edition.
      pages   cm
  ISBN 978-1-62779-187-8 (hardback)—ISBN 978-1-62779-188-5
(electronic book) 1. Men—Psychology. 2. Men—Identity. 3. Masculinity.
4. Man-woman relationships. I. Title.
  HQ1090.K575 2014
  155.3'32—dc23   2014011058

First Edition 2014

Designed by Kelly S. Too

Printed in the United States of America
1 3 5 7 9 10 8 6 4 2

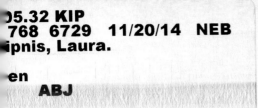
To J.

CONTENTS

MEN

Regarding Men

Men have fascinated me, maybe too much. They've troubled me. They're large and take up a lot of space—space in the imagination, I mean. They force you to think about them. A daddy's girl who grew into a wayward woman, I wasn't that surprised to find, when I started rummaging around in the essays and criticism I'd written over the last fifteen or so years, that it wasn't the random, unsystematic tangle I'd recalled; instead a lot of it seemed to cluster around the subject of . . . men.

What *are* men to me? Rereading led to rethinking, which led to rewriting—it was like taking a cross-country trip to look up old husbands and boyfriends, then setting up housekeeping with a different one every few weeks: getting to say all the things you wish you'd said years ago, admit where you'd been wrong, maybe be a bit more generous (or in some cases, less). They were a pretty motley lot, as you'll see—politicians, pornographers, writers, jocks. . . . Some were slobs, some big loverboys, a few were complete shits. It was odd to realize what a different person *I'd* been with each of them—this one brings out your funny side, this one you're so uninhibited with, this one you could never stop judging and correcting. Writing about someone is a kind of intimacy, after all: as in any relationship there's a lot of projection. It goes without saying that we make other people up according to our own necessities and imaginative horizons, writers no less than spouses, nonfiction writers no less than novelists. What strikes me most about these essays is my covert envy of men, including the ones I would also like to thrash and dismember. Men have always wrested more freedom from the world and I envy that, even when it's a stupid kind of freedom.

Obviously I'm not the only writer in the world preoccupied with men; it's been one of those big literary subjects, most of the time for men themselves. Take Martin Amis, who's said that the most persistent theme in his work is masculinity and opens his own collected essays with a certain mordancy on the subject. Amis is particularly attuned to the specimen he names the New Man, whose appearance he dates from 1970 or so. What's new about this New Man? He makes "all kinds of fresh claims on everyone's attention," says Amis. "Male wounds. Male rights. Male grandeur. Male whimpers of neglect."

No doubt I like this formulation because it weaves my own fascinations into the tenor of our times: I've been writing about men because they forced themselves on my attention. I was walking down the street minding my own business and they grabbed me from behind, Your Honor. Though what's actually most new in Amis's account of the New Man is his self-irony about these masculine travails. When you contemplate the old literary emblems of manhood, they're not exactly insouciant on the subject of male wounds. In the lacking-insouciance camp—and I've lately been rereading many of the bigger guns—Hemingway probably comes first to mind, a writer whose every sentence was scaffolded by such masculine angst he'd be a flattened heap without it; self-irony would be tantamount to yanking out his own vertebrae. In this lineage, the perennially embattled Mailer vies for another top berth, someone else who writes as though castration really was an ongoing threat and not just something invented by Freud. Though unlike Hemingway he could also be quite funny on such fates, antic even: perversely energized by the idea that women wanted to take his pen away, as bemused by the role of phallic avenger as he was committed to it. In the notorious Town Hall debate about women's liberation in 1971, Cynthia Ozick brought down the house by asking Mailer from the audience, "In *Advertisements for Myself*, you said, 'A good novelist can do without everything but the remnants of his balls.' For years and years I've been wondering, Mr. Mailer, when you dip your balls in ink, what color ink is it?" Mailer graciously concedes the round to Ozick, adding that if he doesn't find an answer in a hurry he'll have to agree the color is yellow.

A lot of women find these phallocratic divas insufferable: they take the bluster to heart, or just think them buffoons (Mailer especially suffers this fate—short pugnacious men are easy to mock). But I've always felt more complicated about it. When Mailer pauses in the scabrously hilarious *Prisoner of Sex* to remark of his feminist critics that the best women writers write like tough faggots (he meant it as a compliment), I know I should be stamping my foot along with other offended parties, but I shriek with delight every time I read the sentence. It vibrates with such anxiety, and Mailer wrests such bounty from the condition, he achieves a sort of sublimity.

Of course, it can escape no one's attention that there are as many complaints from women about the New Man as there were about his predecessors: the updated versions of male panic are no less irksome than the old. Today's male is listless, it's said— emotionally paralyzed, indecisive, and insufficiently libidinal, on and off the page. The lack of libido is particularly insulting: male desire may have been a little scummy in its heyday, but if it's on the way out, that would not be exactly satisfactory either. Novelist Benjamin Kunkel, a kingpin of the younger ranks, advises women to go on sexual strike as a protest against male apathy, but . . . wouldn't this be redundant?

In any case, the inevitability of an ongoing mismatch between the sexes is apparently our little tragicomedy to endure, though on the plus side, it makes the other sex so much more alluring. The capacity to be disappointed by someone confers on them a special emotional force, at least as much as being merely gratified. It's an enduring bond. However, my sorties with the natives lead me to suspect that the general advancement from old-style masculine angst to the self-ironies of the New Man has been a lot more jagged than Amis's insouciance or Kunkel's amiability let on. It's those jagged edges—where irony fails and male melodrama begins—that these pieces chronicle.

Something about the poetics of masculine panic, old school and new, just draws me in; these transits between anxiety and excess yank on something similar in my own makeup, I guess. It intrigues me, in a voyeuristic, overly avid way. We've heard a lot over the years about men objectifying women; I offer myself as illustration of the distaff case. But it would be a pretty diminished imaginative life if we were constrained to identify with one gender alone, wouldn't it? I recall once saying in a semi-drunken state to a badly behaved male writer of my acquaintance: "I never know with guys like you, if I want to fuck you, or be you"— which pretty much sums up the situation of a female writer writing about men, I think. By situation, I mean the elasticity of fellow-feeling that stretches to accommodate jealousy, longing, affinity, antagonism, erotics, and every stop in between.

But fellow-feeling aside, men are still a foreign country. The existence of two sexes is the most routine, banal fact of being alive (some would say more than two—not everyone's so easily assignable)—though it's also completely weird. I'm not one of those people who believe in built-in gender differences—that men are rational and women emotional, or other variants on the theme: that way lies cliché. No doubt having different bodies gives us different experiences in the world. But every society in history has also invented a different list of differences between the sexes, and which trait is assigned to which side of the divide keeps changing. Sometimes men are the lusty ones, sometimes women; sometimes men are practical, sometimes it's women, and so on. So a dearth of sweeping theories about the differences between the sexes will be found in the pages ahead (even though I know there's a thriving market for them). But the existence of an "opposite sex" is still pretty riveting—who are these bizarre creatures? These *others*? Masculinity may be a role, but it's no less exotic when you know that.

If the question I should also be addressing in this preface is "Why these particular men?"—why these particular operators, neurotics, sex fiends, and haters (the categories my subjects conveniently grouped themselves into)—it strikes me, rereading these essays, that I keep coming back to a certain kind of man in an involuntary way, like a dog picking up high-pitched whistles. The book is full of disreputable characters: unruly, often a little morally shady. They've stepped out of line, or crossed one, in ways large and small; their relations with women are problematic; there's a lot of emotional chaos and failed self-knowledge on display. There are a few writers who, like me, grapple with their own dubious attractions and repulsions, or are felled by ambition. (There are a few women too, whose relations to men are also especially vexed in some way or other.) As to whether this is a ledger of attractions, aversions, or alter egos, I can only say: all of the above.

So who are these guys to me? "You should of course find the kind of writing in which your pliancy is greatest and your imagination freest," Saul Bellow advises in a letter to someone, and it must be the case that writing about rogues and reprobates made me feel more pliant and unleashed than other available subjects. In the famous Aristophanes tale about love, we're all just severed remnants of our original selves, rummaging among the fragments of other humans for the parts that will make us whole. I suspect it works in a similar way with writers and what they write about. Without vicariousness, without these clashes of attraction and disavowal, would there even be words to put on the page? We're trying to find ourselves in our subjects, or to reconcile with what's missing, even if it's always some version of mistaken identity in the end.

If men writing about manhood are preoccupied with loss—forestalling it, assuaging it, forever dancing around the subject—I suspect that for a woman writing about manhood, it's more of a gain: potency, a bit of lead in your pencil. After all, it's not like women don't have phallic aspirations too! Meaning that at least from the throne of your keyboard, *you* can be the one in the driver's seat, *you* can be the penetrator for a change—I'm speaking symbolically, don't worry—penetrating your subjects with shrewdness and insight, worming your way into their tender psyches, taking unoffered liberties. . . . What I'm saying is that beneath our pleasant façades, women's attitudes toward men are just as rapacious and primitive as the most notorious emblems of hardcase masculinity around. We've just been politer about expressing it—eternally polite. Some have tried to argue, on this basis, that women are possessed of better moral character, but I strongly doubt it. Or I hope not, anyway.

No, the predacious drives and motives are just more submerged. It's what we'd prefer not to know about ourselves that I'm trying to speak of here. As with Hemingway's notorious manslayer shrew-wife Margot, in "The Short Happy Life of Francis Macomber," who accidentally-on-purpose mows down her husband with a big game rifle at the exact moment he finally displays the sort of manliness she'd been mocking him for not having, sometimes your own agenda can come as a nasty surprise.

A writer looking back at a body of work is in a similar position to Margot. Some poor bastard is lying gutshot in the dirt, but your intentions were perfectly scrupulous. (Really.) You find themes and connections that are as impossible to ignore as someone pounding on your forehead with a ball-peen hammer, but it wasn't you who put them there. (Except that . . . maybe—unconsciously—you did.) Having previously written a rather conflicted book on the travails of femininity (*The Female Thing*), I realized only when I got to the end of it that this one is a sort of companion volume. The not-always-salutary ways that men and women figure in each other's imaginations is a theme in both books. Women take men too seriously and not seriously enough, a bipolar condition you'll no doubt find reflected in the chapters that follow. In other words, please don't think I'm offering myself up as some model of progressive or enlightened thinking on the subject of male–female relations—it's probably more like the reverse.

But does a woman writer whose subject is men want to park her buggy only on the enlightened side of the street? Which would mean what? Spending your time protesting that male novelists get more review space than chick lit writers (a recent complaint), or that their characters say dubious things about women and their books don't "get us" (ongoing complaints), and so on? What a boring path to the Promised Land of gender parity that would be. Personally, I'd hate to think that feminism means reforming anyone's weird retrograde identifications or curbing the rapaciousness of fantasy life.

Suffragette or cannibal? I say far better to devour your opponents in a gluttonous frenzy than be fated to earnestness and rebuke-issuing, and the deadly security of what you already know. Introject! Eat them alive! Chew slowly; savor those alarming new thoughts.

I

. . . . .

OPERATORS

The Scumbag

I met *Hustler* magazine's obstreperous redneck publisher Larry Flynt twice, the first time before he started believing all the hype about himself and the second time after. By hype, I mean the uplifting stuff floated in Milos Forman's mushily liberal biopic, *The People vs. Larry Flynt,* and dutifully parroted in the media coverage—that Flynt isn't just a scumbag pornographer, he's also some big First Amendment hero. I liked him better as a scumbag pornographer, though I realize this could be construed as its own form of perversity. Nevertheless, I had a certain investment in protecting my version of Flynt against Forman's encroachments, though, as anyone can see, I was severely outgunned in this match.

The reason we'd met in the first place was that I'd written an ambivalently admiring essay about Flynt and *Hustler,* which the ghostwriter of his autobiography had come across and passed on to Larry, and which he'd apparently admired in turn. The ghostwriter contacted me. I was invited to drop in on Larry the next time I was in Los Angeles, and as it happened, I had plans to be there the following month. A meeting was thus arranged. If I said that getting together for a chat with Larry Flynt was an unanticipated turn of events, this would be a vast understatement. The whole reason I'd written about him so freely was that I never expected to face him in person and could therefore imagine him in ways that gratified my conception of who he should be: a white trash savant imbued with junkyard political savvy. In truth, I found the magazine completely disgusting—as I was meant to, obviously: it had long been the most reviled instance of mass-circulation pornography around and used people like me (shame-ridden bourgeois feminists and other elites) for target practice, with excremental grossness among its weapons of choice. It was also particularly nasty to academics who in its imagination are invariably prissy and uptight—sadly I'm one of this breed too. (A cartoon academic to his wife: "Eat your pussy? You forget, Gladys, I have a Ph.D.")*

Maybe I yearned to be rescued from my primness, though Flynt was obviously no one's idea of a white knight. (Of course, being attracted to what you're also repelled by is not exactly unknown in human history.) For some reason, I tend to be drawn to excess: to men who laugh too loud and drink too much, who are temperamentally and romantically immoderate, have off-kilter politics and ideas. Aside from that, it also happened that in the period during which my ideas about things were being formed, the bawdy French satirist Rabelais was enjoying an intellectual revival in my sorts of circles, along with the idea of the "carnivalesque": the realm of subversion and sacrilege—the grotesque, the unruly, the profane—where the lower bodily stratum and everything that emerges from it is celebrated for supposedly subverting established pieties and hierarchies.

---

* For the record, I teach filmmaking (though eventually became more interested in writing than in shooting films myself), so am actually a bit on the margins, academically speaking. (So I like to tell myself.)

I was intrigued by these kinds of ideas, despite—or more likely because of—my aforementioned primness. Contemplating where one might locate these carnivalesque impulses in our own time I'd immediately thought of *Hustler*, even though back then I had only the vaguest idea what bodily abhorrences awaited me within its shrink-wrapped covers (as if a thin sheet of plastic were sufficient to prevent seepage from the filth within). In fact, the first time I peeled away the protective casing and tried to actually read a copy, I was so disgusted I threw it away, I didn't even want it in the house.

Eventually steeling myself against my umbrage, I mounted another attempt. *Hustler*'s assaults on taste and decency were indeed echt-Rabelaisian, I quickly saw, as even a partial inventory of its pet subjects will indicate: assholes, monstrous and gigantic sexual organs, body odors, anal sex, farting, and anything that exudes from the body—piss, shit, semen, menstrual blood—particularly when it sullies public, iconic, or sanctified places. Not for *Hustler* the airbrushed professional-class fantasies that fuel the *Playboy* and *Penthouse* imaginations. Instead, *Hustler*'s pictorials featured pregnant women, middle-aged women (denounced by horrified news commentaries as "geriatric pictorials"), hugely fat women, hermaphrodites, amputees, and—in a moment of true frisson for your typical heterosexual male—a photo spread of a pre-operative transsexual, doubly well endowed. In short, the *Hustler* body was a gaseous, fluid-emitting, embarrassing body forever defying social mores, and threatening to erupt at any moment. A repeated cartoon motif was someone accidentally defecating in church.

Basically, *Hustler*'s mission was to exhume and exhibit everything the bourgeois imagination had buried beneath heavy layers of shame, and as someone deeply constrained myself, whose inner life has been shaped by the very same repressions and pretensions

Hustler is dedicated to mocking, the depths of its raunchiness often seemed directed at me personally. Reading it I felt implicated and exposed, even though theoretically I'm against all those repressions too. At least I *wanted* to be against them.

I immediately embarked on reading as many back issues of the magazine as I could locate. These were generally to be unearthed in the discount bins at the back of neighborhood porn stores—this was back in the pre-Internet days, when people had to actually leave their homes to procure porn. Hunting down old copies of *Hustler* became for a while my weekend hobby, the way some people go antiquing or collect Fiesta ware. Poring over my growing bounty of issues, I could see that *Hustler* was definitely upholding a venerable, centuries-long rabble-rousing tradition of political pornography, though it still completely grossed me out.

I wasn't completely unaware of the irony involved in surveying *Hustler* from this somewhat rarefied intellectual vantage point, especially given how allergic the magazine itself is to all forms of social or intellectual affectation, squaring off like a maddened pit bull against the pretensions (and earning power) of the educated classes. That it was so often explicit about its class resentments reassured me that there was more going on than just raunch for its own sake, though its politics could also be maddeningly incoherent, with its arsenals of vulgarity deployed at American leaders and public figures on *every* side, systematically sullying *every* national icon and sacred cow. Of course it ranted against the power of government, by definition corrupt; dedicated countless pages to the hypocrisy of organized religion, with a nonstop parade of jokes on the sexual predilections of the clergy, the sexual possibilities of the crucifixion, the scam of the virgin birth, and the bodily functions of nuns, priests, and ministers; and especially despised liberals (along with, needless to say, feminists), all epitomes of bourgeois conventionality in its book.

Yet the magazine was also far less entrenched in misogyny than I'd assumed. What it's against isn't women so much as sexual repression, which includes conventional uptight femininity, though within its pages, not everyone who's sexually repressed, uptight and feminine is necessarily female: prissy men were frequently in the crosshairs too. In fact, *Hustler* was often surprisingly dubious about the status of men, not to mention their power and potency; often perplexed about male and female sexual incompatibility. On the one hand, you certainly found the standard men's magazine fantasy bimbette: always ready, always horny, up for anything, and inexplicably attracted to the *Hustler* male. But just as often there was her flip side: the leagues of women disgusted by the *Hustler* male's sexuality—haughty, rejecting (thus deeply desirable), upper-class bitch-goddesses. Class resentment was modulated through resentment of women's power to humiliate: "Beauty isn't everything, except to the bitch who's got it. You see her stalking the aisles of Cartier, stuffing her perfect face at exorbitant cuisineries, tooling her Jag along private-access coastline roads. . . ." Hardly the usual compensatory fantasy life mobilized by typical men's magazines, where all women are willing and all men are studs, as long as they identify upward, with money, power, and consumer durables.

Once you put aside your assumptions about *Hustler*-variety porn aiding and abetting male power, you can't help noticing how much vulnerability stalks these pages. Even the ads play off male anxieties: various sorts of penis enlargers ("Here is your chance to overcome the problems and insecurities of a penis that is too small. Gain self-confidence and your ability to satisfy women will skyrocket," reads a typical ad), penis extenders, and erection aids (Stay-Up, Sta-Hard, etc.). The magazine is saturated with frustrated desire and uncertainty: sex is an arena for potential failure, not domination. You don't get the sense that the *Hustler* reader is feeling particularly triumphal about his place in the world; that these guys are winners in the sexual caste system.

I wrote up my somewhat conflicted thoughts about *Hustler*'s pornographic truths and Flynt's self-styled war against social hypocrisy, and though I took a somewhat sardonic approach to both, I suppose I ended up kind of a fan. A nation gets the pornography it deserves, which is obviously why so many people are affronted by it. Once the essay came out I kept getting requests to write more about pornography, which was irksome because I was never all that crazy about any of it, Rabelais notwithstanding. Still, I guess you could say Flynt turned out to be kind of an influence in my life.

So there I was, a self-appointed expert on all things *Hustler*, seated across from the founding father himself in his thickly carpeted penthouse emporium atop the huge kidney-shaped office tower on Wilshire Boulevard, the one with his name emblazoned on the roof in towering letters that you can see for miles. If the magazine is a battleground of sex and vulgarity, Flynt's office was no less an assault on the senses: Tiffany lamps dueling with garish rococo furniture, gold and velvet-covered clashing everything—it looked like armies of rival interior decorators had fought and died on the job. The surprisingly charming Flynt presided over this expensive-looking mishmash from his famous gold-plated wheelchair (a long-ago assassination attempt by a professed white supremacist enraged by *Hustler*'s interracial pictorials had left him paralyzed from the waist down*). All those years in the

---

* Joseph Paul Franklin claimed responsibility for the shooting though was never tried for it. He did receive multiple life sentences and a death sentence for other racially motivated killings.

chair have given him an extreme case of middle-aged spread: his face has a melted quality, with only a hint of the self-confident cockiness from old pictures. Newly image-conscious with Forman's biopic about to be released, he told me immediately that he was on a diet. "I may be a cripple, but I don't have to be a fat cripple," he chortled hoarsely.

This helped break the ice, though I was still in a state of mental confusion, faced with this large, damaged, flesh-and-blood man in place of my theoretical construct. On the one hand, I felt like I knew him intimately, having spent so much time conjuring him in my imagination and then crafting him on the page, but at another level everything was also unbridgeable between us. He, of course, had spent no time imagining me, I assumed, though he did pronounce my essay on him "feisty." This pleased me a little too much—I wanted his good opinion, yet I also wanted not to care about what he thought of me. I also wasn't sure if by "feisty" he meant the various potshots I'd taken at him in print or just that I'd bucked received feminist wisdom about the magazine, which had not exactly been popular in those precincts.

He wanted to correct me on one point, he said. I'd repeated what I'd read elsewhere—that the shooting and surgeries had left him with no bowel or urinary control, an ironic fate for a man who'd built an empire offending bourgeois sensibilities with their horror of errant bodily functions. To compound the ironies, this man who'd raked in millions on the fantasy of endlessly available fucking was also left impotent—or so I'd written. Flynt said it was the only thing I'd gotten wrong: he'd never been impotent. This seemed like rather intimate territory given the brevity of our acquaintance. I said I'd take his word for it.

Having cleared that up, we talked more easily about my essay and his magazine, then he invited the ghostwriter (also in attendance) and me to tag along to a private movie screening up in the

Hollywood Hills. Which we did, and afterward trailed Larry and his small entourage to a late-night deli in Beverly Hills. He was gracious and congenial, but I never lost the double consciousness of feeling I was accompanying a character sprung from the recesses of my own fantasies.

This feeling was compounded when the ghostwriter sent me an advance copy of the autobiography a short time later. I was taken aback yet, I have to admit, gratified to find that passages I'd written about *Hustler* had been inserted into Larry's mouth as his first-person account of himself. Another passage, followed by my name, had been excerpted and reproduced on the back cover in the form of a blurb, just below the ones by Oliver Stone and Milos Forman.

I mention this to explain why my attitude toward Flynt may have a certain proprietary quality: it's because I *invented* him. Or let's say I invented a version of him that I found palatable, and he went along with it. If only other men I've known had been so compliant. (Isn't this one of the main factors in relationship failure, by the way: other people not conforming to your idea of who they should be?) Though I never really got the impression Flynt had a very firmly fixed idea about who he was in the first place; I suspect he's more of a scavenger when it comes to identity, which was fine with me. I just wanted him to stay the way I'd fantasized him.

Which, as I've mentioned, was a lot different from the way film-maker Milos Forman fantasized him.

Pained liberalism is the predominant sentiment in *The People vs. Larry Flynt*. Pornography may be a necessary evil, but Forman personally dislikes it and wanted it known, once the movie was released, that he'd never personally purchased a copy of *Hustler*. On my part, I at least sat down and forced myself to read the thing. I may have been disgusted by Flynt but I was willing to learn from him; Forman was all about teaching Flynt an etiquette lesson. The result is a masterfully made movie that sanitizes Flynt's cantankerous, contrarian life and career into one long, noble crusade for the First Amendment, while erasing everything that's most interesting about the magazine, namely the way it links bourgeois bodily discretion to political and social hypocrisy. The movie reeks of class condescension. I bristled on Larry's behalf, though needless to say he was basking in the attention, mostly worried about his waistline and promoting the upcoming autobiography.

For Forman, Flynt's story was about "becoming an American, a politically cognizant citizen"—as though he wasn't one to begin with. It may have been Czech émigré Forman's love letter to American democracy, but it's also a stunningly undemocratic one if it turns out that political cognizance is the province of the educated classes and Flynt has to learn good citizenship at the feet of his betters. As he does here, under the tutelage of his lawyer, Alan Isaacman (a composite of Flynt's many lawyers over the years, as he required a small army of them)—predictably, the character with the most education becomes the movie's moral center.

The movie does at least dramatize how ready a nation founded on the principle of free speech was to back up its codes of social propriety with storm troopers: Flynt is variously gagged with electrical tape, carted off to jail for disrupting courtroom proceedings, and sent to a psychiatric prison for smart-mouthing a judge. To the sober-sided Isaacman, Flynt's behavior is simply crazy: why would a sane person defy the law? Probably because for Flynt it was just another scam. It thus became his compulsion to locate every loophole he could in the nation's obscenity laws, and use them to taunt his fellow citizens; his favored tactic being to systematically and extravagantly violate, in the grossest way possible, each and every deeply held social taboo, norm, and propriety he could find.

Failing to appreciate the neo-Rabelaisian inventiveness, the nation responded with its knee-jerk response to all perceived insults and injuries: the lawsuit. Flynt was endlessly clapped in jail on obscenity charges brought by the state, and spent upwards of $50 million over the years defending himself against the hundreds of civil suits brought by his outraged targets. Then there were the contempt charges. Flynt loved playing the wild man in official settings, and in the years following the shooting, his public behavior became even more bizarre—in constant pain, he'd become addicted to morphine and Dilaudid, finally detoxing to methadone. He famously appeared in court sporting an American flag as a diaper and was arrested; at another trial, described by the local paper as "legal surrealism," his own attorney requested permission to gag his unruly client. On one of his Supreme Court pilgrimages, Flynt got himself arrested for shouting at the justices, "You're nothing but eight assholes and a token cunt!"

It's one of the all-time great lines in the annals of uncivil disobedience, but Forman despises these bad-boy theatrics; Flynt's dissidence makes him uncomfortable. Instead, for him the hero of the story is the Supreme Court (he's said as much in interviews). Flynt only deserves our respect when he starts kowtowing to the state: proper citizenship in this movie means obeisance and sucking up to power; freedom means the freedom to conform. When Flynt finally behaves himself and shuts up for the first time at the landmark Falwell libel trial, *that's* the film's moment of triumph. When Isaacman beams approval at Flynt for finally acting like a grown-up, tears welled in my eyes—that's how adept Forman is at peddling this pap. Repackaging Flynt's raunchy career into a tribute to American tolerance, wrapping it up in Hollywood's favorite narrative cliché, personal growth—it's exactly the kind of syrupy sentimentality *Hustler* always ridiculed. But so what—you're going to leave the theater snuggled in a big, warm self-congratulatory glow, whether you want to or not. Look how great we are! Long live America! Lost amidst the flag-hoisting is the awkward fact that *Hustler*'s entire reason for existing was to crap on this sort of national self-idealization.

Of course, as Forman himself said, he'd never actually read the magazine. His contempt for it leads him to miss the crux of the story: the hero wasn't the Supreme Court. It's been pornography that's pushed the boundaries of political speech ever since the invention of print. The interesting paradox is that as long as political and religious authorities keep trying to suppress them, obscenity and blasphemy will always be wonderfully effective ways of mounting social criticism. Flynt didn't invent the tactic, though he did use it to leverage his unique brand of anti-authoritarianism into an empire.

Please don't think I'm mounting an argument for liking *Hustler*—quite the opposite. The existential dilemma of obscenity is that it requires our inhibitions in order to be effective. So let's hear it for sexual propriety and shockability, which were, among other things, Flynt's ticket out of grinding rural poverty—born in Magoffin County, Kentucky, then the poorest county in America, the son of a pipewelder, Flynt is very much the product of the white trash demographic the magazine supposedly addresses. From Magoffin County to Beverly Hills: if anyone owes a debt to sexual repression, it's Larry Flynt, though you might say the same of Freud too, who built a nice little career for himself on similar foundations.

. . .

I imagine the dilemma for anyone who's had a movie made about his life is whether you end up consciously or unconsciously transforming yourself into the movie's version of you. After Forman's film converted Flynt from loathsome pariah to chubby-cheeked media darling, after he watched Manhattan's glitterati coo over his supposed life story at the closing night of the New York Film Festival and was jetted to Czechoslovakia with director Forman to screen the movie for fellow dissident Václav Havel—after Flynt chose Forman's version of him over mine, in other words—what was to become of him and his unbeloved magazine?

Hoping to capitalize on the buzz from the movie, Flynt issued his ghostwritten autobiography, *An Unseemly Man: My Life as Pornographer, Pundit, and Social Outcast*, shortly later, another attempt at repackaging his life story in an audience-soothing way. Yes, it's sprinkled with bestiality, sybaritic sex, drugs, and vulgarity, but more often it's the new, "improved" Larry Flynt sauntering through the pages: waxing patriotic, spouting platitudes—"America is the greatest country in the world because it's the freest"—and analyzing himself in the upper-middlebrow idioms of pop psychology.

After all those years of using the national stage as a public toilet, now Larry wants our love? His version of his life was as sappy as Forman's.

When I met up with him next—he was visiting Chicago on a publicity stint for the book—he was still floating in a post-biopic bubble, which I found myself wanting to puncture. I asked him if it felt weird to be receiving so much media adulation—did he resent people trying to clean him up, to make him palatable to middle America? He said, "What's weird isn't getting all the attention now; what felt strange was being so vilified for all those years."

The vilification had indeed been pretty intense. Even after the assassination attempt, the country's reaction was barely sympathetic. Flynt had made a national nuisance of himself, like some attention-grabbing overgrown adolescent boy mooning the guests at a church social, and the general attitude was that he more or less got what he deserved. News reports of the shooting took a sardonic tone: *Time* billed it "The Bloody Fall of a Hustler." The thing worth saying, though, is that unlike your run-of-the-mill pornographer, Flynt's own body has been on the line too, including, it turned out, as a sacrifice for America's long history of racial pathology. That Flynt, who was regularly accused of racism, was shot and paralyzed by a white supremacist outraged about *Hustler*'s liberality on interracial sex—another sensitivity the magazine trod upon long before it was an unremarkable thing— was another twist in an exceedingly convoluted story.

Still in bubble-puncturing mode, I told him I thought the movie had sanitized him too much. He readily agreed, but added earnestly, "If the First Amendment can protect even a scumbag like me, then it will protect all of you, because I'm the worst." It was a mawkishly noble sentiment, and also a line directly from Forman's movie script—hearing it from both "real" Larry and movie Larry, I cringed on each occasion.

Or maybe I'm being too hard on him. Who can hold out forever against the malign forces of conventionality? No doubt my Flynt was every bit as fabulated as Forman's; still, it was painful to hear him saluting the flag instead of using it as a diaper, and parroting the film's banalities. I couldn't help thinking that America hadn't been content with simply paralyzing Flynt, it had to finish the job by reconfiguring him as a patriot and then dousing him in approval for finally growing up. *That's* how they get you, I thought darkly. Even lowlife pornographers are suckers for love and a place in the history books, it turns out, lifting a pudgy cheek to the breeze when the world is blowing kisses their way.

We talked on the phone a few times after that—I was attempting to interview him for a magazine piece, but given my lack of skill at it, the interviews mostly devolved into chats. He liked to introduce his body into the conversation, I noticed and was never exactly sure how to respond—I could only think of it as a tragic deadweight, a thing best left unmentioned. He announced with pride that his most recent diet had been a great success: he'd lost thirty pounds. "Trying to make yourself more sexy for the ladies?" I asked lamely. "Nah, I just looked at myself in the movie [he has a cameo role as a judge] and saw how fat I was, and I said, 'Who wants to be a porker like you?'"

Falling back on feminist prosaicisms, I tried goading him about how he'd like having the spotlight turned on himself instead of it always being women's bodies on display. "How about a Larry Flynt centerfold?" I asked. He answered immediately, "The reason more men don't want to take their clothes off is because they're so uptight about their little dicks. In all the X-rated videos and magazines they're twice the size of a normal penis and it's given every man in America a complex. Even though women all tell me that as long as a guy knows what he's doing, size isn't that important."

I said that women are trained to lie to men, though I wasn't sure he got the sarcasm. "Women have the same problem about their breasts as men have about their penises," he assured me. "If someone could somehow get men and women on the same wavelength about this breast–penis thing, I think it would do more to enhance everyone's life than anything else." It was a rather utopian vision, coming from a scumbag pornographer.

Since then I've followed Flynt's exploits from a distance, watching as he's evolved into a sort of elder statesman–pornographer, weighing in unpredictably on national matters and civil liberty issues. When his would-be assassin, Joseph Paul Franklin, was about to be executed in Missouri in 2013 for killing a man outside a synagogue in 1977—just one of at least twenty race-related murders he'd been convicted of or implicated in—Flynt filed a last-minute motion through the ACLU to halt the execution. He was against the death penalty, he announced, and didn't believe the government should be in the business of killing people for vengeance. Franklin was executed anyway, amidst a national controversy about whether the drugs employed in the lethal injection cocktail would cause him to suffer. Flynt, who after years of brutal pain finally had the nerves leading to his legs cauterized to stop all sensation, said he'd love to spend an hour in a room with Franklin inflicting the same damage on him that he'd inflicted on Flynt, but didn't want to see him die.

A couple of years earlier I'd been contacted about blurbing his latest book, *One Nation Under Sex*, a coauthored account of the sex lives of American presidents throughout the nation's history. I labored to come up with a good quote and finally arrived at this: "Larry Flynt has waged a lifelong battle against hypocrisy and prudery, shattering every propriety and slaughtering every sacred cow. The political classes have never been safe from his special brand of satire. Now he turns his rabble-rousing sensibility back though time with a similar imperative. No more whitewashing! Smash decorum! Bring down the elites!"

I was happy to be in touch with him again, even through

intermediaries. He'd meant something to me—he made me examine my limits, he'd challenged me at my corked-up core. I liked the idea that he still thinks about me, as I do about him. I imagined myself giving him a call the next time I was in LA, but I suspect it won't happen.

The Con Man

Every woman adores a con man—to steal a page from Sylvia Plath. Especially one who knows you better than you know yourself, who looks into your eyes and reads your dirty secret desires, who knows what a bad girl you really are under the prim professional façade, and then takes you for everything.

Such a man is "Mike": sleek, a reptile, but a sexy reptile, the kind you hate yourself for wanting to fuck. He exudes confidence, as a con man should. "I want to see how you operate," Dr. Margaret Ford tells him the second time they meet, and she sure gets what she asked for. She wants to *write* about him, she says, to *study* him for a book or article, but it's pretty clear what she's really come back for. "You want to see how a true bad man plies his trade?" he banters knowingly. "Plies his trade" should be understood as a euphemism.

I don't expect many people will recognize the setup of David Mamet's 1987 *House of Games*: it didn't exactly kill at the box office and isn't part of anyone's twentieth-century film canon, though it pulled down a handful of foreign awards. But most moviegoers probably have a film or two filed away in the "hated it but can't stop thinking about it" category, catalogued thus not because of any intrinsic merits or demerits, but because it cuts too close to home. It tells you something about yourself you'd rather not know, or something about the world you don't want to accept. If I say that the storyline of *House of Games* involves an overly cerebral woman spying on a bunch of sleazy but sexy men and then getting her comeuppance, possibly you can see why *House of Games* would be a movie that makes me nervous.

A deeply repressed psychiatrist, Margaret Ford is the author of a pop-psychology bestseller, *Driven: Compulsion and Obsession in Everyday Life*. There's something off-putting about her from the minute she strides into the frame: with her barbershop coif, stubby nails, no-nonsense gait, and boring businesslike suits, she's denuded of all the conventional attributes of femininity—asexual or mannish, take your pick. Worse, she's so humorless—when she smiles, only her mouth moves; the rest of her face is immobile. As played by Lindsay Crouse in a stiff, stagy, mannered performance, it's like watching an articulate piece of wood. (As it happens, Crouse was married to writer-director Mamet at the time the movie was made; they divorced three years later. If the way he directed her in this role wasn't one of the grounds, it should have been.) Dr. Ford needs you to be aware of her elevated place in the world—you see it in the hoity-toity way she brandishes her professional competence, which is irritating. Then there are the small hypocrisies: supposedly an expert on compulsion, she's a workaholic and a chain smoker herself, obsessively scribbling data about her patients in notebooks while trailing Freudian slips behind her like a piece of toilet paper stuck to a shoe. "Physician, *hear* yourself," you want to say.

But it wouldn't help. This lady shrink is such a stranger to her own desires that she's lured into acting out her own humiliation

in an elaborate con game orchestrated by an ensemble of charismatic con men whose perfect understanding of the female unconscious lets them play her like a jukebox. It doesn't help that
she's the least self-knowledgeable shrink on the planet, which
is—though I am not any sort of shrink myself and would even
agree that your average psychotherapist is not, as a matter of
course, exactly neurosis-free or especially self-acute—a joke I take
to heart nonetheless. In fact, the movie accrues many such jokes at
its protagonist's expense. Consider the overabundance of vehicular
symbols—"Ford," "Driven . . ." from which an automotive-age
Freud would likely deduce a condition of being stuck, stalled,
fixated—thus compelled and doomed to neurotic suffering. Which
is, indeed, the small jest that motors *House of Games*.

Things first start to go south when one of Ford's patients,
Billy, a compulsive gambler, pulls a gun and threatens to shoot
himself in the middle of a session. Ford coolly bargains with
him: "Give me the gun, and I will help you," she says confidently.
"You don't do dick, man, it's all a con game, you do nothing," he
taunts. Nevertheless, a suddenly docile Billy hands over the gun
along with a challenge: he owes twenty-five grand he doesn't
have to a guy named Mike—"the Unbeatable Gambler, seen as
Omniscient," according to Ford's notes—and they're going to
kill him if he doesn't pay up the next day.

"Give me the gun and I will help you" is the first of a series
of exchanges Margaret Ford enters into with men, exchanges
that take the form: "You give me something and I'll give you
something." The problem is that she so overestimates her bar-
gaining power that you're embarrassed for her. She's negotiating
with counterfeit currency—her professional expertise, soon her
sexuality—though she won't find out what a fraud she is until
way too late. A problem of equivalences haunts the story—what
does Ford have that's equal to that gun? Not one thing.

Nevertheless she marches straight over to the House of Games, a seedy pool hall–bar with a backroom poker game, striding in like she owns the place. (Psychotherapy consumers in the audience will be laughing bitterly into their popcorn, accustomed as we are to the brutal finitude of the fifty-minute hour.) *"What the fuck is it?"* Mike (Joe Mantegna) demands, strolling onscreen, backlit as a man of mystery should be. When he steps into the light, the first thing you notice is how good he looks in that suit, if maybe a little slick—you can practically smell his aftershave wafting into the theater. "You think you're a tough guy, I think you're just a bully!" Ford upbraids him on her patient's behalf, after telling him why she's there. Apparently impressed with her mastery of the situation, Mike compliments her on her skills of perception. "How'd you size me up so quick, that I'm not some hard guy who's going to rough you up or something?"

"Well, in my work . . ." she begins.

"What is your work?" he naturally inquires.

"None of your business," she tells him tartly, all business.

Okay, we've been here before: the heiress and the gangster, the lady and the vulgarian she cuts down to size with her classiness and poise. Ford demands that Mike cancel Billy's debt, which occasions the film's second exchange, this one initiated by him. He'll tear up Billy's IOU if Ford pretends to be his girlfriend and spies on another player in a high stakes poker game. (*Pretend to be his girlfriend?* You already know she's dying to.) What she's supposed to look for is a "tell" that this player is bluffing. A tell, as Mike explains it, is a behavior that gives something away. Margaret herself has a tell—she gestures with her nose toward the hand in which she conceals a chip, meaning he can read her secret correctly every time, as he proceeds to demonstrate. In other words, he can see her in ways she can't see herself, which is a sexy quality in a man.

Now installed in the back room in the role of Mike's girl-friend and drawn in by her seeming ability to discern the other gambler's ostentatious tell, she offers to stake his hand with a personal check for six grand at a crucial point in the game. Suddenly things get tense, the other gambler brandishes a gun ... which on closer view appears to be leaking water. Whereupon Margaret retrieves her check, whereupon all the players chuckle and break frame—ah, they'd been setting her up, turning her into a mark. The whole poker game had been staged to con her out of her money.

"It was only business ... nothing personal," says Mike, unperturbed, handing her a chip. "Here's a souvenir of your escape from the con men." This elicits an actual smile from Ford—a crack in the façade, *finally*. When she laughs she's a different person, like the uptight secretary who suddenly lets her hair down, though Margaret's hair is too short to either put up or let down. "You're a lovely woman," Mike murmurs meaningfully later that night, all oleaginous charm, putting her in a cab. And bidding him good-night, in the soft glow of the streetlight, she suddenly does look a lot less like an iceberg.

What a great move: letting Margaret see them trying to con her and failing to; letting her think she's outsmarted them. Flattering her intelligence, inviting her into their club—giving her a little tour of their world, schmoozing over late-night sand-wiches—oh yeah, she's *one* of them now. These guys are so good at what they do they can see five steps ahead; predict Ford's every response while letting her think *she's* the one in the driver's seat.

What Ford doesn't know (nor does the audience at this point, because we're *all* being taken for a ride) is that Mike and his merry band of con artists are so skilled in textual hermeneutics that they've managed to discern from a close reading of Ford's bestsell-ing advice book that there's a pathological aspect to the author's nature that will make her *want* to be their victim. The screwed-up Dr. Ford doesn't just *write* about compulsive behavior, she's so afflicted by some little-understood compulsion of her own that she's practically begging to be taken, in all senses of the word.

Having caught the bad men in the act, hubristically thinking that her savvy inures her to their wiles, Ford returns to the House of Games in search of Mike. She has a "proposition" for him, she says. She wants to write a study of the confidence game, and she wants him to cooperate. Mike readily agrees, and another exchange is initiated. But what's in it for him? Just the implied quid pro quo—the double entendre of the "proposition"? Indeed, after the first evening's tutorial, Ford follows him to a hotel, where he cons his way into an out-for-the-evening stranger's room, adding to the evening's illicit thrills. They go to bed, and afterward she's suddenly quite lovely, eyes sparkling, in softer focus (we also see that she was wearing pretty lingerie under the mannish outfit—yup, she knew how the evening was going to end when she got dressed). On the way out she slips a lighter from the bureau into her purse as a souvenir, as though bedding Mike had unloosed something a little delinquent in her.

Then somehow, like in a bad dream, they run into Mike's pals and she finds herself swept up in another con, this one involving a briefcase containing eighty grand in cash, supposedly borrowed from the mob. Things go awry, someone gets killed, the briefcase goes missing, and *uh-oh*, Mike's in big trouble—the money's due back the next day. Ford, thinking *she's* the one who screwed it up, maybe even got the guy shot, heads to her bank to withdraw eighty grand from her own account and save the day. (Courteously, the con guys drive her there.) She hands over the money, still not realizing that the con *was on her* all along, though by this time the audience is catching up. But how could she fail to put two and two together, even after Mike had said pointedly during one of his tutorials, "Everybody gets something out of every transaction"? Or, when back in the hotel room and Margaret, mooning around in a post-coital glow, had mused, "Some people would say you're an interesting man," and he'd said coldly, "I'm a criminal. I'm a *con man*. You don't have to delude yourself."

Avoiding self-delusion: here's a useful life lesson for all of us, though easier said than done, self-delusion being pretty much the definition of the human condition. Ford's finally jolted back to reality when, suspicions aroused, she follows her patient Billy and spies on a scene she's not meant to see: Mike and his con men pals divvying up her money, the eighty grand she'd beneficently come up with to repay the mob. "Mike, how'd you know she was going to go for it?" one of them chortles. "Go for it? The broad's an addict," he answers. "Took her money and screwed her too," someone compliments him. "A small price to pay," he smirks.

When in the film's tense climax Ford confronts Mike face-to-face, meting out justice at the end of a gun (Billy's gun, the one she'd taken off him earlier, in classic MacGuffin fashion), suddenly we're in a female revenge plot, an artier *I Spit on Your Grave*. But even after Ford plugs him with a bullet, Mike's not backing down from his diagnosis: that getting rooked was what she *wanted*. "Hey, fuck you," he spits at her, wounded and bleeding. "You crooked bitch . . . you thief . . . you always need to get caught—'cause you know you're bad. . . . You sought this out. . . . I knew it the first time you came in. You're worthless, you know it. You're a whore." (He pronounces it "hoor," like an old-style gangster.) She tells him to beg for his life but, his own man to the end, he won't. *Bang, bang, bang.* She shoots him dead, while he writhes and twitches on the floor. But she's killed off the film's most charismatic character and you can't help disliking her for it—the screen just seems empty without Mike around.

The shooting temporarily evens the score—a brief moment of purifying revenge, with Ford finally refusing to play the dupe. But it's a hollow triumph—Mike *was* right all along, as we see in a sort of coda when Ford reappears, following a long vacation. She's transformed! Her hair has highlights, she's wearing something splashy and floral, dangly earrings grace her ears. When the newly feminized, lip-glossed doctor is asked to sign a copy of her book by a fan, she inscribes it, "Forgive yourself"—an earlier bit of advice from her mentor Maria, another female shrink. At the restaurant where she's meeting Maria for lunch, she surreptitiously boosts a fancy lighter from another woman's open purse, a small smile of satisfaction playing on her lips.

So . . . everything she'd been repressing—her femininity, her klepto tendencies—have been unleashed by blowing Mike away with a handgun? She finally knows who she is? This appears to be the conflicted logic of the denouement. On the one hand, killing Mike kills the messenger who'd delivered the painful self-knowledge about what a worthless crooked bitch she is; on the other, her newfound self-acceptance has miraculously cured her of whatever stick was up her ass. Yeah she's a crooked bitch, but she's okay with that.

Why does this movie enrage me so? (Why have I also watched it countless times?) Maybe because it's Mamet's little joke on brainy women everywhere: our instincts are shot—too much book learning has left us denatured and floundering, unable to survive in the real world (or the "real world" Mamet invents to bludgeon us with). When Ford finally gets a brutal self-education at the hands of the all-seeing con men, note that their instincts are pretty much infallible. Still, to the extent that Ford embodies all the arrogance of medical science, you're not crying crocodile tears for her as she gets herself rooked. She's kind of an asshole, swaggering around with her advanced degrees and hefty checking account—no problem walking out of a bank with eighty grand on demand, I noted with envy.

But the decks are also so stacked against her. The world of the con and the world of psychiatry would seem, at first glance, like entirely different enterprises, yet the sleight of hand *House of Games* pulls off is staging an epistemological contest between the two and conning us into buying it. Here, the con isn't just a criminal operation, it's a codified system of knowledge passed down through the generations; the con men are a *guild*, practicing and refining their technique. Indeed one of the pleasures of the movie is its lessons in the mechanics of various cons ("The Mitt," "The Tap," etc.), and learning how to scam people out of their money orders. We feel, like Ford, flattered to enter their world, and a little more wised up about the hazards awaiting the unwary.

The knowledge base of psychiatry isn't quite as romanticized, even though as interpretive methods go there's actually a curious similarity between them, at least in Mamet's conception. Consider the "tell"—as Mike explains it, it's a lot like what Freudians call a parapraxis (slips of the tongue, the pen, or other unconscious but "telling" behaviors). Except that here it's the con man who's expert at analyzing people's desires, not the clueless shrink. All Ford has are stupid theories out of books; she couldn't interpret her way out of a paper bag. Mike's knowledge is appealing and sexy; hers is antiseptic. He holds Margaret's hand and can tell which finger she's thinking of; later, when he propositions her, he knows what she *really* wants. "You're blushing. That's a tell. These things we want, we can do them or not do them, but we can't hide them."

At least you can't hide them from Mike, the movie's epistemological hero. The film sets up an interesting philosophical tension between seeing and knowing, but it's a fixed race from the start. Ford sees, but she sees in useless ways, because she doesn't *know herself*; she doesn't know what her experiences mean. In each exchange, someone's withholding a crucial piece of information—namely, where she really fits into the story, which is as a mark. Not knowing her place makes her ridiculous.

But it's not the con men setting her up, it's the film that makes her a dupe. As it does us in the audience—we're dupes too. Or we're dupes as long as we know only what Ford knows, which leaves us languishing in the feminine boondocks along with her. When the "aha" moment finally comes—for us ahead of Ford—that she's been *had*, and everything she (and we) thought she'd done of her own volition (including bedding Mike) was scripted in advance by the all-knowing con men, at least we get to trade feminine ignorance for masculine competence, which comes as a relief, because who wants to be a sucker?

It's this fantasy of male infallibility that becomes a little annoying. Note that psychiatry and the con are gender-segregated spheres here: there are no female con artists; there are no male psychiatrists. The one other shrink we meet—Ford's mentor Maria—gives her the stupid advice to stop working so hard and go find some "joy"—"Do something that gives you satisfaction!" Look where *that* gets her. It's not only ways of knowing the world that are gendered in Mametland, it's epistemological competence overall. Here's a world, not so unlike our own, in which knowledge is power; but if only men are granted knowledge, women are natural born losers. To say this is a fabulously misogynistic film is an understatement, but it's a version of misogyny that's so pleasurable and cleverly orchestrated that I find myself loving every minute of it. (Then hating myself in the morning.)

Obviously Ford's fate worries me: I know how susceptible I am to having my intelligence flattered; at least it's worked often enough in the past. Would I have been able to hold out against a guy like Mike? Doubtful. You know he's no good—he practically has a sign on his forehead. But I bet Margaret isn't the only brainy female around to have been drawn to an overconfident guy with an edge of wrong. You want all my money? Let me write you a check. Make it out to cash? No problem. I once dated a gambler semi-briefly (it's possible there was later some recidivism). He knew the world of backroom games and their habitués, which seemed exotic to me; he had theories about reading the flop and when to play tight versus loose, skills I thought could prove useful in life, not that I play poker. At dinner one night he flashed a huge wad of cash, several inches thick; he'd been in a high stakes game the night before. I riffled through it—mostly hundreds. One side of me thought, "How crass," but another side was thrilled. He had a shifty sort of charm and could calculate the odds of drawing to an inside straight off the top of his head. A lot of things he told me about himself didn't quite add up (including that he was pathologically honest), but I could overlook it.

It's what Ford overlooks about Mike that paves the path to catastrophe. But she looks into his eyes and feels recognized; she feels like he knows her secret places. Now, this is a perennially powerful idea in the female romantic imagination—the man who knows you inside and out. There's something thigh-tingling about it. Isn't it why women fall in love with their shrinks? Not because anything about them is actually so enticing (usually the reverse—they sit in armchairs all day and get big butts); it's the

way they penetrate your inner life that's seductive, their knowledge of your soul and related organs. "And what is it you think I
want?" Ford asks during the seduction scene. "What am I?" When
Mike shows her that he knows what she desires, that he knows
her *there*, it's the first time Ford registers as desirable—at least
according to the conventions of female desirability that movies
have attuned us to for the last century or so—because for the first
time, she's *penetrable*.

The woman penetrated by a man's knowledge *is* a perennial
movie motif; also why repressed neurotic females make such useful protagonists. It's no accident that Ford makes all those Freudian slips. Symptoms are a dialectic of the visible and the invisible:
something is buried or repressed, and needs to be uncovered. As
Mary Ann Doane explains in *The Desire to Desire,* discussing
1940s-era medical melodramas focused on the emotional and
physical illnesses of female characters, this buried thing requires
the appearance of another character: the revealer-of-what-is-
hidden. Typically it's a male doctor or psychiatrist, summoned to
cure the female lead by revealing some secret truth and, along
the way, curing her resistance to her femininity. *House of Games*
at least modernizes the contrivance: the repressed female is herself a shrink, and the surrogate shrink is a con man. And here the
diagnosis isn't exactly a curative.*

---

* The diagnostician also doesn't have to be a doctor. In Hitchcock's *Marnie,*
another movie about a repressed kleptomaniac, it's Marnie's former boss, the
handsome department store heir Mark Rutland, who steps into the role, forcing
the frigid Marnie to marry him, then raping her on their honeymoon. This turns
out to be therapeutic though, because he also forces her to confront her buried
traumatic childhood memories and since it's Sean Connery in his prime doing the
raping (and it all happens offscreen), it doesn't seem like the *worst* thing in the
world. I was once asked by a feminist film historian doing some kind of survey to
name my favorite sex scene in a movie and said the first thing that came to mind:
"The honeymoon scene in *Marnie.*" She made a peculiar snorting noise with her
sinuses; I felt mortified for years whenever I ran into her.

But it's something about Ford's repressed desires that makes her a mark: somehow these brilliant con men have discerned from her buttoned-up demeanor not only that what she *really* wants is to be spontaneous and wanton and fuck strangers in hotel rooms, but also that she'll fall for their rickety scam. *"Do you think you're immune from experience?"* demands one of her patients. Ford denies it, which is Mamet's clever little trap for her. If she's closed to experience, she's dried-up and frigid. But opening herself to experience gets her royally screwed. Either way she loses. I understand that Mamet isn't trying to represent the entirety of the female condition (at least I imagine he'd deny it if asked), and there's no reason to take the movie as some sort of parable or pronouncement, but if it resonated with me more than it should, and in ways that I really do completely fucking resent, I suppose it's because for women of my generation—post–sexual revolution, post–second wave feminism (third wave? fourth?)— erotic recklessness and going places you shouldn't was supposed to be our right if we chose to claim it. If we wanted to get in on some of that sexual adventurism guys have always taken for granted, whose business was it?

Except that here, going to the wrong side of town for thrills makes you into a dirty joke for a bunch of sniggering men. After she and Mike have sex and Ford steals the lighter from what she thinks is a stranger's bureau—well, it turns out it was Mike's, part of the set dressing concocted for her benefit. "The bitch boosted my lucky lighter," Mike complains later on to the gang. Much jocularity and hooting: "The bitch is a booster," one of them confirms. "The bitch is a born thief." When they steal, it's business; when she steals, it's smutty, some variety of female perversion. "So you had her made from the jump," someone congratulates him. More levity all around. *"Took her money and screwed her too."*

Hearing this rather blunt assessment is what spurs Ford to revenge. "You learned some things about yourself you'd rather not know," Mike says brusquely later, when she's waving her gun at him. What she's meant to have learned is that you can only con people who want to be conned, people like her for whom being taken advantage of fulfills some subterranean yearning. That's Mike's credo anyway. Technically she hadn't even been conned, she'd sought out the chance to confirm her deepest pathologies. And she's sexually ridiculous to boot: "What are you gonna tell 'em, Stud?" he mocks her, when she threatens to go to the cops. I'm not sure which would be worse, losing eighty grand or being so ruthlessly diagnosed.

Reversing Billy's accusation that she doesn't "do dick," Ford does what dicks do the world over: abuse power, even though it's only with Billy's gun that she acquires the requisite equipment. So, having taken care of business like so many beloved movie vigilantes before her, what's next for our score-settling heroine? As in the classic medical melodrama denouements where the cured heroines blossom, getting pretty clothes and doing fancy things with their hair, she graduates into full-blown femininity. Having strolled into the House of Games thinking she could be one of the guys, she emerges by film's end cured of all feminine ambivalences.

So dead as he is, Mike wins the epistemological contest anyway. Sure he was a con man, but he's still the character most identified with truth in this movie; he may have lied for a living, but at least he wasn't lying to *himself*. Whereas Margaret . . . "You raped me," she accuses Mike, waving her gun around. "You took me under false pretenses." Really?

"You asked me what I did for a living, this is it," he says jocularly, just before she plugs him with a bullet. But easy for him to say—*his* inner life was never under scrutiny; *his* sexuality was never penetrated by the movie's narrative apparatus. It's not diagnosing his sickness that's been the fulcrum of the story—not what cheating people gratified in him, or whether he was anxious about performing in bed with Ford. . . . From any evidence of his inner life or unconscious conflicts the film looks discreetly away.

Though I truly hate it when people say about movies "That wouldn't really happen," as though they're supposed to slavishly emulate reality (they're not), I can't help wanting to ask: *do* con men read self-help books about compulsive behavior and brilliantly distill buried psychological truths about their authors? How *does* Mike so adeptly predict Margaret's every move in advance, down to the minute, which he'd have to for the setup to work? Obviously if you think about any of this too much, it crumbles into fairy dust.

The better question isn't whether it's realistic, but whether it's convincing. If the whole narrative contraption hinges on male omniscience, a lot of mystification is clearly required, and the audience has to be willing to be seduced by the pretense—as willing as Margaret was to be duped by Mike. But I'm game. It's wonderfully easy to be lulled into Mamet's either/or universe, even when you *know* that the world he pays tribute to, the one dictated by the desires of men, is already an anachronism; that his planetary system is lit by a dying sun.

But if this movie still deals men the winning hand . . . well, so has history, for most of existence. Now, *that* was a long con. Mamet parlays the foul emotional truth about life under the ancien régime into an elegantly seductive storyline. Who is the enigmatic and seductive Mike? A stand-in for the way those historical residues are still lodged in women's (and everyone's) psyches: for the fantasy about the man who knows you better and more deeply than you know yourself. I love/hate this film because it knows me so well, fissures and all. It seduces me all over again every time I watch it.

The Trespasser

It's worth choosing the right muse if you're in the market for one—having the right muse can make all the difference. Though it's not entirely clear if *choice* is precisely what takes place. Impulse? Instinct? Probably the whole business isn't rational to begin with—who knows what recesses of the psyche are engaged. Still, when someone else's muse propels him to riches and fame, it makes you wonder if maybe you yourself failed at the muse-choosing thing somewhere along the way. Yet being overly aspirational regarding muses can also prompt social rebuke, as when a not-especially-lovely man fastens on one of the most elegant women in the world to serve in this capacity. Some will find it ambiguous as to whether this is classical or creepy, especially in cases when the two aren't exactly social equals. And when the man in question isn't exactly an artist.

"A curious, grunting sound": this was the noise emitted by celebrity stalker–photographer Ron Galella whenever he consummated a shot of—or more precisely *at*—the object of his long-standing obsession, Jacqueline Kennedy Onassis, as she testified during one of their numerous courtroom encounters. You can imagine her delicately wrinkling her nose while saying it. It can't have been pleasant being trailed everywhere she went by this hairy lug thrusting his equipment in her face. Everything you need to know about Galella is that *he* was the one who instigated the lawsuit rather than Jackie: not content to merely hound her, he also sued her for $1.3 million, claiming that Secret Service agents (assigned to protect the Kennedy kids) were preventing him from doing his job. Which, as he construed it, involved trailing the former First Lady whenever she left her Fifth Avenue apartment and squeezing off shot after shot while crooning her name. When Jackie countersued, claiming that he was terrorizing her, he at least got to be in the same room with her, on the same footing, which had to be gratifying. What did it matter that he ended up saddled with a restraining order since, true to form, he gleefully violated it, arranging for himself to be photographed while doing so. Posterity beckoned, Ron had the film. He eventually got the judge to knock the restriction down from fifty yards to twenty-five feet on appeal, then violated that too. "You stay away from me or I'll see you in court again," Jackie hissed, and he made sure she did. So there they were together for one more round, practically side by side—the publicity gods were smiling down on Ron once again.

If you get the idea that Galella was a little driven in his pursuit of Jackie, this wouldn't be wrong. But obsession is the mother of invention, and Galella was nothing if not inventive in his quest to capture Jackie on film. He dated her maid to get the lowdown on her household habits; he bribed her doormen to find out when she was leaving her apartment, then tailed her all over town in taxicabs. He disguised himself in wigs and fake mustaches, showed up at funerals and the theater, and leaped out from behind coat racks at fancy restaurants to capture her startled-doe expression. He even managed to track her down at her children's Christmas pageants. Once, on an outing in Central Park with the kids, she finally lost it—finding Galella hovering around yet again she bolted, dashing into the foliage like a startled fawn. There went Ron galloping after her, snapping away at her elegant retreating form like a great white hunter chasing wild prey.

When asked why he was so obsessed with Jackie, as he increasingly was—he was getting pretty well known for his antics and, of course, the lawsuits—he'd say that he saw himself as performing a public service. A mumbling Bronx-born gum-chewer and, let's face it, not the world's most eloquent guy, he became positively heartfelt when speaking of Jackie: dogging her wherever she went was just what he was put here on earth to do. Not that he didn't enjoy the notoriety, and getting to be a bit of a celebrity himself. The Jackie fixation rescued Galella from being just another putz with a camera: ironically, it's what made people start to take him seriously. For those who see neurosis as the origin of creativity—and it's a fairly common cultural conception—what better artistic bona fides than a public idée fixe? It implied that he had a rich inner life, which is what we require from our artists; it notched him upward in the cultural pecking order. The *National Enquirer* days were behind him—not that he ever refused to sell his work to anyone, but these days his photos are at the Museum of Modern Art and he's featured in collections around the world. These are more impressive venues than guys in his line of work—though he wears the label "paparazzo" proudly—generally aspire to.

But Jackie wasn't the only recalcitrant subject. His quarry ranged from Greta Garbo (hiding her face behind a handkerchief) to Mick Jagger (giving the finger to the camera) to Sean Penn (punching out Galella's paparazzo nephew). Galella especially liked getting pix of the most reclusive stars—Hepburn,

Brando—staking them out for hours, days if he had to. He was the most dedicated of pests: he once got exclusive photos of Taylor and Burton by camping out in a rat-infested attic for an entire weekend with a quayside view of a yacht across the street they were scheduled to board days later. They all *tried* hiding from him, without success—Hepburn, crouched behind an umbrella, scuttled away like a sandcrab, others pulled their coats over their heads like criminals on a perp walk, but images of hounded stars are salable too. Yes, many found Galella to be a king-sized pain over the years, not that it troubled him.

Maybe it's this supreme lack of shame that gives his photos such a compelling immediacy. "Look over here! Look over here!" he'd beseech, using a nickname or anything to draw the victim's attention, and often capturing something unstudied in these familiar faces, wresting something "real" from a world of over-managed surfaces. His most famous shot, of a windswept Jackie, glancing back at the camera with a half-smile, has an undeniable aura— it's hard to take your eyes off her. Galella calls it his "Mona Lisa," though he readily admits that Jackie only smiled because he disguised his voice, and she didn't realize he was the one hailing her.

The term "paparazzo" derives from the name of one of the swarming photographers in Fellini's *La Dolce Vita*, though it's also supposedly a play on the Italian word for the annoying buzzing of a mosquito. One thing you can say about Galella is that he never shirked the physical hazards of being an annoyance. Marlon Brando knocked out five of his teeth when Galella wouldn't stop photographing him; Galella sued (he called his lawyer before he called a doctor), settling for 40K—the amount it cost him to reconstruct his jaw, minus a third for the lawyer fees. Which didn't prevent him from once again lying in wait for Brando following a benefit at the Waldorf-Astoria, though this time he wore a customized football helmet emblazoned with his name. Mindful of his own increasing legend, he made sure to have himself photographed trailing the reclusive stone-faced star through the lobby.

Having reached his eighties, Galella has been racking up the tributes lately, with shows booked well into 2015, proving that annoyances who stick around long enough eventually become cultural darlings. No doubt he deserves some credit too as a forerunner of today's 24/7 celebrity harassment—yes, he should get a mention in the history books for that wonderful feat. But let's talk about this salvage process that hoists professional vulgarians who sprout a few gray hairs into respectability, rebranding them as benign and lovable figures. You see it happening all over the place these days: another renowned aggressor-against-proprieties, the scatological countercultural cartoonist R. Crumb, has been the subject of countless museum retrospectives and tributes too. Why can't thorns-in-sides just keep on being thorns-in-sides—do they have to get adoration for it too? It's disheartening to watch the former cultural nuisance join in his own rehabilitation, so moved by all the love that he forgets to thumb his nose at the niceties he used to abhor. He begins speaking of his artistic process, his childhood, his personal demons, and fitting his story into the over-familiar templates and sanctimonies his career was once devoted to smashing.

It was the same thing with professional thorn-in-the-side Larry Flynt, rehabilitated by Milos Forman's biopic. In fact, Galella too has been the subject of a loving film treatment by an award-winning director, the 2010 documentary *Smash His Camera*, by Oscar winner Leon Gast (*When We Were Kings*). It's an enjoyable film, but the clanking of the cultural elevation machinery is a little deafening. It premiered at the Museum of Modern Art fittingly, given the artistic burnish Gast confers on Galella, opening with him in the darkroom swishing his prints around in developing fluid like a latter-day Stieglitz. Galella happily plays along, throwing himself into the role of an aging paparazzo-auteur, leading the film crew to the sites of his most famous Jackie shots and letting them trail him to a photo shoot, though he doesn't actually do that kind of thing anymore. You can see why. This one's a stage-managed red carpet event featuring Brad and Angelina—press passes required—and Ron can barely get a clear shot of them through the thicket of other paparazzi, his soulless spawn, with their press credentials and digital cameras.

The film feigns evenhandedness about its subject—diehard elitist and former Metropolitan Museum of Art director Thomas Hoving is trotted out to denounce Galella as an "obscene bottom-feeding so-called journalist"; others brand him everything from a parasite to a sociopath. On the "Is it art?" front, Gast gathers a collection of photographers and photo editors to sit around a table and squabble about Galella's artistic legacy: does his work have something going for it beyond his famous subjects, or is he just a second-rater who'll be forgotten fifty years from now?

It's Jackie who's brought in to settle the question—if she was his muse, then Ron is an artist. Or maybe she was more than muse? "It was a relationship conducted through the camera, but it was nevertheless a personal relationship," contends a former *Life* magazine editor. Galella "captured something that was very elusive about Jackie," gushes gossip columnist Liz Smith. "He loved her," lyricizes magazine editor Bonnie Fuller. "And he loved her children." Both Jackie and Ron benefited from "this push-me-pull-me thing," Smith adds. "In the end, she was posing for him—she must have had a little feeling for Ron."

Here things take a turn toward the sentimental and plummet into sheer mythology, though it's a myth Ron's apparently come to believe in himself. He too speaks about Jackie as though they were entwined in something deep together. When the film attempts to probe Ron's innermost feelings about her, he's happy to help. Why did he have this obsession with Jackie? he's asked. He says earnestly that he's tried to analyze it: It was because he had no girlfriend at the time. He wasn't tied down or married, so "she was my girlfriend in a way." (Those bouts of self-analysis don't seem to have been too taxing.)

The film is more successful at sounding his inner life when it proceeds less directly. After Onassis brought Galella back to court for repeatedly violating the restraining order and he was threatened with six years in prison if he didn't desist from photographing her for the rest of her life, it seemed he might be forced to finally abandon the fixation. But no one ever abandons a true fixation; we just find creative work-arounds. When Ron first spoke on the phone to his future wife, Betty, a photo editor, her voice reminded him of Jackie's, he recalls: soft and sort of whispery, a laughing sort of voice. They arranged to get together, and he proposed marriage within the first five minutes of meeting her. She said yes. They went to the nearest motel to consummate the deal (he says), and have been happily married ever since. Betty also handles the business end of things.

Their mansion in Montville, New Jersey, makes the Sopranos' place look modest, its indoor acreage a monument to the world's insatiability for celebrity images. The warehouse-sized basement is devoted to the massive Galella archive—aisle upon aisle of floor-to-ceiling industrial shelving holding literally millions of Ron's photos, with a staff to monitor the illnesses and deaths of celebrities, making sure to have prints on hand whenever one shuffles off the mortal coil, or seems about to. The grounds of the place are lavish too, replete with Italian gardens, columns, burbling fountains and windmills—and an array of spray-painted silk flowers and polyurethaned topiary, lovingly planted by Ron himself. ("It's an utter and absolute humiliation," says Betty, whose parents were florists.) Ron is also strangely obsessed with rabbits and keeps them as pets. "They're cleaner than cats," he explains. "They don't smell. And when you pick up their poop it's like raisins." Gass provides a cute montage of Ron rolling around in bed with a few of his cuddly friends. Rabbit memorabilia is strewn throughout the mansion, and out back there's a private cemetery for pet rabbits past, replete with a sculpture garden of bunny statuary—including the famous Bugs—some as big as full-grown men.

What's with all the fucking bunnies? It's one thing to sublimate aggression and violation into art (or even "art"), it's another to transform them into kitsch and cuddliness. All this cuteness about the bunnies and flowers is overdone, as though rebranding Galella as Mr. Quirky will be good for his legacy. I get that transforming a photo archive into an oeuvre means convincing us that there's a consciousness behind the work, one with depth and interesting contours, meaning Ron needs to be set apart from your usual hired-gun magazine photographer out on assignment. An oeuvre is the product of a sensibility, whereas the other thing's an industrial product. And art is worth a lot more, monetarily speaking, than celebrity journalism. Understood; we just don't need all this sensibility jammed down our throats.

It's not that I begrudge Galella whatever cultural respect anyone wants to confer on him. Ron learned photography in the Air Force, then went to a commercial art college, while I went the fine arts educational route, where we learned early on to nurture our obsessions as the path to cultural respect. It was never precisely stated but simply understood that your obsessions were your bread and butter, your ticket to eventual gallery shows, and, someday—hopefully before you were too old to enjoy it—reverential articles in *Artforum* and the attendant perks. The more obsessed you were, and the more committed to your weirdness, the more seriously people took you, especially the instructors.

I was doing some photography in those years too, though I never really mastered the technical stuff like exposure. For my final project in one class, following the tracks of my weirdness, I did something that in retrospect seems bizarre but proved to be the ticket to unimaginable success. I was living in San Francisco's Mission District, which also served as a landing strip for squadrons of the homeless and deinstitutionalized (though at the time they were still known as bums and winos), and somehow got the idea of asking one of these neighborhood habitués to come home with me and having him dress in my clothes, then photographing him for an installation project. There was an accompanying sound track I'd written and recorded on the theme of brief encounters and dashed romantic illusions. The piece was called *Brief Encounter*.

I paid him of course, and he was pretty amiable about the whole thing, though looking back I don't know what I was thinking. I showed the piece to an influential visiting artist who was doing critiques of student work. She pronounced it unethical and reprehensible but also made a phone call that got me invited to a prestigious fellowship program in New York for budding artists—I'd passed the "Is it art?" test with flying colors apparently—which eventually led to a grad school fellowship, then another fellowship, and then a teaching job. Looking back, I guess the homeless guy was sort of my Jackie.

What's odd about it all isn't just the happenstance of how careers get off the ground, it's realizing how much the themes of that piece continued to haunt my work, even after I drifted away from the art world and started writing books. When I came across the script for the piece in a box of papers from those years, there were lines almost identical to some in a book about love I'd write twenty-five years later. Things turned out okay, I guess; still, I wonder whether Ron's choice of muse was a little more propitious than mine. What does it say about our respective inner lives that his was a famously gorgeous woman and mine a local wino?

But that visiting artist was right: we exploit our muses and it's not a two-way street. It's what Gast and Galella's other partisans resist acknowledging—they're eager enough to designate Ron an artist, yet want to sentimentalize away the aggression and egotism of art and make him cuddly. But it's not exactly evident that being an artist and being an upstanding guy were ever one and the same thing.

Some of the Jackie images, out of his many thousands, were included in a 2012 retrospective of Galella's work in Berlin—the exhibit is still traveling around Europe, speaking of artistic success—and in the sumptuously produced volume *Ron Galella: Paparazzo Extraordinaire!* that accompanied the show. Replete with admiring essays by a bevy of German critics, it's a beautiful object in its own right: two hundred gilt-edged pages each the weight and thickness of shirt cardboard; 104 gorgeously printed black-and-white images with a running commentary on Galella's antics over the years. Though many of the original images were actually color, the lush black-and-white confers more artistic gravitas, which seems to be the idea. But that gilt-edged paper tries too hard—it's gravitas jammed down your throat.

Ron is determined that he and his muse will go down in history arm in arm: his website, which advertises a new collection called *Jackie: My Obsession* (available for $300, or in a limited edition for $2,000), asserts rather gracelessly that "our collective memory of Jackie would be non-existent if it weren't for Ron Galella." But graceless or not, posterity is still calling, and Ron's there with the prints.

Juicers

I struggle with an embarrassing affliction, one that as far as I know doesn't have a website or support group despite its disabling effects on the lives of those of us who've somehow contracted it. I can't remember exactly when I started noticing the symptoms— it's just one of those things you learn to live with, I guess. You make adjustments. You hope people don't notice. The irony, obviously, is having gone into a line of work in which this particular infirmity is most likely to stand out, like being a gimpy tango instructor or an acrophobic flight attendant.

The affliction I'm speaking of is moral relativism, and you can imagine the catastrophic effects on a critic's career if the thing were left to run its course unfettered or I had to rely on my own inner compass alone. To be honest, calling it moral relativism may dignify it too much; it's more like moral wishy-washiness. Critics are supposed to have deeply felt moral outrage about things, be ready to pronounce on or condemn other people's foibles and failures at a moment's notice whenever an editor emails requesting twelve hundred words by the day after tomorrow. The severity of your condemnation is the measure of your intellectual seriousness (especially when it comes to other people's literary or aesthetic failures, which, for our best critics, register as nothing short of moral turpitude in itself). That's how critics make their reputations: having take-no-prisoners convictions and express-ing them in brutal *mots justes*. You'd better be right there with that verdict or you'd better just shut the fuck up.

But when it comes to moral turpitude and ethical lapses (which happen to be subjects I've written on frequently, perversely drawn to the topics likely to expose me at my most irresolute)—it's like I'm shooting outrage blanks. There I sit, fingers poised on key-board, one part of me (the ambitious, careerist part) itching to strike, but in my truest soul limply equivocal, particularly when it comes to the many lapses I suspect I'm capable of committing myself, from bad prose to adultery. Every once in a while I suc-ceed in landing a feeble blow or two, but for the most part it's the limp equivocator who rules the roost—contextualizing, iden-tifying, dithering.

And here's another confession while I'm at it—wow, it feels *good* to finally come clean about it all. It's that . . . once in a while, when I'm feeling especially jellylike, I've found myself loi-tering on the Internet in hopes of—this is embarrassing—cadging a bit of *other* people's moral outrage (not exactly in short supply online) concerning whatever subject I'm supposed to be addressing. Sometimes you just need a little shot in the arm, you know? It's not like I'd crib anyone's actual *sentences* (though frankly I have a tough time getting as worked up about plagiarism as other people seem to get—that's how deep this horrible affliction runs). No, it's the tranquillity of their moral authority I'm hoping will rub off on me. I confess to having a bit of an online "thing," for this reason, about *New Republic* editor-columnist Leon Wieseltier—as everyone knows, one of our leading critical voices and always in high dudgeon about something or other: never fearing to lambaste anyone no matter how far beneath him in the pecking order, never fearing for a moment, when he calls someone out for being preening or self-congratulatory, as he frequently does, that it might be true of himself as well. When I'm in the depths of soft-heartedness, a little dose of Leon is all I need to feel like clambering back on the horse of critical judgment and denouncing someone for something.

I suppose some will condemn me for taking these shortcuts. I know the whole idea is that your moral outrage springs from some authentic place deep within the fibers of your *own* superego, and you're not supposed to be enhancing your performance with artificial supplements cribbed from the Internet.

These remarks are prefatory to admitting that, having gone the mother's little helper route on occasion myself, I find it especially difficult to pass judgment on the increasingly long list of those suspected of, or admitting to, juicing their game in some way or another too. I wish I could work myself into a lather about it—I realize the consensus view is that juicing is a moral affront. They hold Senate hearings on it, for God's sake. But frankly, I'd rather juice than slip down in the rankings too. Like so many other ambition-wracked bastards, I'll do what I have to when it comes to staying competitive.

But men have it far worse when it comes to staying competitive at the moment. They've *lost* it, apparently: their edge is gone, they're lumpish, unemployed, and increasingly obsolete. Or so it's been reported, notably by Hanna Rosin in a much-lauded magazine article with the guillotine title *The End of Men* (later expanded into a bestselling book). "What if modern postindustrial society is simply better suited to women?" asks Rosin provocatively. Patriarchy may have been the organizing principle up until now, but the era of male dominance is finally over, largely because eighty percent of the jobs lost in the last recession were lost by men (prompting the jokey term "man-cession") and, according to Rosin, men aren't bothering to retool sufficiently to find new ones. We all know about declines in traditionally male industries like construction and manufacturing (of course, capital crushing the labor movement was part of the job loss story, too). The good news for women is that the information economy doesn't care about your size and strength, which were men's sole advantages in the past. What's needed today is *social intelligence*. Also obedience, reliability, and "the ability to sit still and focus"—traits seen by employers as women's particular strengths. Which is why women are procuring the largest percentage of what few jobs remain, and are now, for the first time, a majority of the workforce.

One notes a certain mocking tone on Rosin's part when it comes to men getting thrown under the employment bus. They've lost, we've won: hooray for us! But maybe the triumphalism is a bit myopic, given that it was the ruthlessness of winner-take-all capitalism that chewed men up and spit them out when their services were no longer necessary (then the so-called jobless recovery kicked them in the nuts for good measure). Sure it's the new social reality, but is it really anything to crow about?

And maybe women have been a little *too* adaptable? Yes, the job market has flipped toward us; yes, we now hold more of the cards—except, unfortunately, when it comes to heterosexual women who want some kind of equal partner as a mate, or any mate at all. With men transformed into soft-bellied unemployable losers, more and more women are left high and dry in the romance and mating department. One option Rosin offers is for men to become the wives while women go to work. The problem with this scenario, as Rosin herself acknowledges (though only in

passing), is that these new jobs women are procuring aren't especially high-paying. The dirty little economic secret of the last
forty years is that the job market played women off against men
to depress *everyone's* pay.* Which is to say (though Rosin doesn't)
that the real winners when it comes to the influx of women into
the job market during this period have been our capitalist overlords. Still, why assume, as Rosin seems to, that it means the
overlords should get to dictate the terms of the social bargain?

This is why I'd like to suggest—returning to the juicing epi-
demic and my own propensity for situational ethics—that playing by the rules of whatever industry currently employs you may
once have been a premise with some moral force, but now it's
just obtuse. That's how you get rooked. If women are more
employable these days because bosses like how well we play by
the rules, allow me a moment of appreciation for some good old-
fashioned rule-breaking of the sort men have had more opportunities to perfect, as emblematized by the long parade of big-time
juicers ritually hung out to dry in the media.

Take Major League Baseball star pitcher Roger Clemens
(indicted for perjury and obstruction of Congress after his testi-
mony denying steroid use), cyclist Lance Armstrong (stripped of
his seven Tour de France titles for doping), the embattled A-Rod,
or any other sports world miscreant of your choice. But I'm also
thinking of juicers closer to my own professional neck of the woods,
namely authors of factually dubious memoirs such as James Frey,
publicly indicted for lying about his past in his 2003 bestselling
memoir, *A Million Little Pieces*. To refresh your memory, Frey
was the former junkie who produced a swaggering account of

---

* Not much of a surprise, since the same dynamic has been unfolding on a global
scale too, with cheaper labor abroad used to punish overly demanding workers at
home.

self-destruction, criminality, drug addiction and valiant recovery, though it turned out that he'd made up a lot of the best parts. This is supposedly verboten in the memoir-writing business, though the perimeters of the genre have been (as with doping, until recently) selectively observed at best. Or there's Mike Daisey, the political monologist who massaged some of the details in *The Agony and the Ecstasy of Steve Jobs,* his theatrical piece about the gruesome labor conditions at Apple's Chinese manufacturing plants, saying (when exposed) that it was dramatic license.

Like Clemens and the rest, Frey and Daisey illicitly boosted their games too, by employing prohibited substances—not anabolic steroids or EPO, but fictional experiences in supposedly nonfiction genres. Now, none of these guys is any sort of prince, apparently: Clemens is, by all accounts, a major jerk; Armstrong lied about doping for years while suing and maligning anyone who tried to tell the truth; and about A-Rod, the less said the better. Frey was given to bouts of eye-rolling braggadocio and self-regard, and let me add that I was never a fan of his writing despite thinking he'd been turned into a scapegoat for the publishing industry, which has always talked out of both sides of its mouth about memoir factuality, especially when it comes to commercial blockbusters. As for Daisey—well, he trades on liberal guilt, which is the worst thing I can find to say about him. Let's leave him aside.

They may be problematic characters, but none of them were talentless schlubs either. No one got where he did on sheer fakery. What they did was augment the talents they had to stay competitive. The aging Clemens wanted to eke out a few more playing years—a few more wins, maybe a World Series, before being tossed out to pasture. Frey, an aspiring writer, wanted to publish a novel, which he submitted to seventeen publishers. No one would buy it, though when he mentioned that it was based on his own life, he got offers—an unknown recovery memoirist is a more commercial prospect at the moment than an unknown first-time novelist, even when it's basically the same story. For Clemens and the rest of the jocks, the problem is that bodies aren't indestructible; for Frey it was that he actually wasn't enough of a reckless law-flouting desperado to satisfy the addiction-memoir readership's demand for life stories that read like novels but are packaged as nonfiction. So they tweaked their games to meet the performance demands of their industries. In Rosin's language, they retooled.

Which brings us to another knotty issue: ambition. Now, I don't wish to obscure the essential obnoxiousness of possessing overly copious amounts of the stuff, but what a lot of hypocrisy attends this subject! Please be aware that when I speak of ambition's excesses, I offer myself as a prime example, which no doubt explains why I'm so guiltily fascinated by contemporaries who've been raked over the coals for their immoderacy. Still, my question is, who decides how much is *too* much?

As we know, modern market societies require ambition, because they're premised on social mobility, which is essential to a flourishing democracy. Ambition is a social good because we believe in growth and innovation, and meritocracy is supposed to promote such things. This is our modern religion. The problem, of course, is that ambition is distributed a lot more liberally than talent or ability. The founding principle of democratic society is *supposed* to be that your position in the world derives from your capacities and achievements, not your origins: call it the myth of the "level playing field." But the painful truth is that talents and capacities are just as inequitably distributed as noble birth once was—there's no democracy of talent, there's no equality of ability. Those not lucky enough to have been blessed with one or the other are just out of luck, and headed for the lower ranks in a system like this one.

But even for the lucky few favored with some quantity of talent, it has to be the *right sort* of talent for your particular time and place. Meaning that in a market society, it has to be a monetizable sort of talent, because talent is only measured according to what someone's willing to pay you for it. In other words—to return once again to myself—a talent for wishy-washiness is no talent at all in a critical "meritocracy" based on ruthless moral severity.

I mean, how come when they were handing out moral seriousness, Leon Wieseltier got so much and I got so little? What kind of level playing field is that? Even for those with relatively modest ambitions, how can you not resent people who rise faster or further based on genetic flukes or temperamental happenstance? Why them, not you? Frankly, if they distilled moral seriousness and sold it in dime bags, I'd be shooting it up like there's no tomorrow, until I was bristling about everyone else's moral bankruptcy and intellectual shabbiness too, just like my steely ego ideal (who not so long ago won the half-million-dollar Dan David Prize for his achievements in cultural standard setting, by the way—speaking of monetizing your talents).

From where I sit, it's not difficult to see how the ambition-afflicted keep falling in the soup of professional scandal. We're just trying to rectify life's inequities—maybe boost our position in the world a notch or two by patching up the weak spots, where necessary: a bit of muscle mass here, some dramatic incident there, or whatever it takes. Sure, anxious types get over-zealous: inventing degrees, fudging scientific data, cribbing sentences, and onward into ignominy. Transfusing your own blood to win a bike race *is* a little creepy. But when I think about what I'd do to boost my performance, I can't get that judgmental. And let's not forget the tens of millions who can't get through the day without *their* little performance enhancers: the Prozac, the Viagra, or whatever you take to sleep at night to be on top of your game tomorrow.

So basically, when I look at the juicers, the boosters, and the fakers, moral relativist that I am, I see hopeful strugglers and stragglers just trying to get some love back from the world. Like me: I fake certainty and strong opinions, whipping myself into a high fury about every last thing, since if I didn't, who'd want to read what I write, and going unread is not exactly going to get *me* any love from the world. Oh, maybe I'd get a crumb or two if I played clean, but for all of us whose ambitions exceed our present status in the world, it's never not depressing that someone's invariably getting more than you.

Also, there's another inequity to contend with that I'd like to mention. Why is "doing whatever it takes to win" excessive for an Armstrong competing in the Tour de France, but not for his former corporate sponsors when *they* do what it takes to win: outsourcing jobs to sweatshops abroad (thank you, Mike Daisey, for the reports) or whatever their insatiable drive for love—I mean, obscene profits—demands? Why are individuals supposed to uphold some antiquated pre-capitalist code of honor when their employers and industries honor nothing in return? They definitely don't reward loyalty—it's not exactly breaking news that players wreck their bodies to cultivate a 95-mph fastball, then get put on waivers when their value drops for owners. Or take everyone's favorite liar, James Frey, who was apparently supposed to thrust aside commercial pressures in a grand romantic gesture, because it was up to him alone to singlehandedly contest the momentum of global capitalism and the corporatization of publishing.

There's a curious anti-capitalist romanticism in the finger-pointing at juicers, even from those who have no gripes at all with the market system otherwise. You find this sort of thing a lot at the movies, where turning down money is a sign of integrity (the "You can't buy me" moment—always amusing to see the highest-paid stars playing heroes who can't be bought). At the same time there's quite some reverence for the superrich—the tech-bubble billionaires, the self-promoting real-estate magnates with strange hair—to whom we turn for life lessons and character tips. Our relationship to capitalism is rather schizophrenic, in other words, though it's no mystery why. Apart from a few iconoclasts who live off the grid or the lucky few who live off inherited wealth, we're all tailoring ourselves to marketplace logic in ways large and small: hoping to get an edge, find an angle, raise our games. Yet in the contemporary moral-monetary equation, market-driven behavior is coded as "selling out"—it makes you a whore. *"He's such a whore,"* someone's always proclaiming righteously about the coworker or friend who's been a bit too visible about self-marketing, *too* much of a kiss-up to the boss. Frey: a major publishing whore, everyone said. Linguists call this "therapeutic slang"—a way of letting ourselves off the hook for our own weaknesses or hypocrisies. It's the language of self-exoneration: denying awkward truths by tossing the ball to someone supposedly worse. (Also not very fair to actual prostitutes, who end up doing double duty, linguistically speaking—shouldering the burden for everyone's self-hatred about peddling our wares in the marketplace too.) But no one ever said that negotiating the emotional fallout of life in a market society was an easy business.

I'm all for anti-capitalist romanticism, though one doesn't wish to become a moral poseur in its service. Poseurs have immutable principles and categorical imperatives at their disposal, coupled with vast certainty about their own capacities for integrity. They use other people's public foibles as an opportunity to fantasize about how admirably they'd behave in circumstances they've never actually faced. Of course, moral relativists are no less fantasy-prone: we fantasize that the world will someday stop blaming individuals for the systemic inequities they find themselves battered down by. We wish to point fingers at the structural determinants of behaviors that moral poseurs want to hang on individuals alone. Some of us also overidentify with scofflaws and boat rockers, not all of whom are nice people. Whereas the poseurs are content to simply cut them down to size, and luckily for them, there's always another delinquent on the public chopping block for one thing or another.

Recently an email arrived with the subject heading "Plagiarism," which I opened immediately, heart in throat, assuming I was being accused of it. I was already plotting my Doris Kearns Goodwin defense (plead shoddy notetaking, follow with private settlement), but it turned out, my correspondent informed me, that someone with the enviable name of Lianne Spiderbaby, who reviews horror movies—and was on the cultural radar because she's successful, attractive, and dating Quentin Tarantino—had been caught lifting sentences from other people's writing and including them in her reviews. Despite the relatively mundane level of this transgression it was the Web scandal du jour, at least in that particular subcultural corner, and may have even put the kibosh on Spiderbaby's forthcoming book deal. Initial reports were that Quentin had been set to write the foreword, but the publisher dropped the book. The publisher tweeted that the author herself had withdrawn it, then deleted the tweet. Spiderbaby tweeted an apology to her fans, then deleted that too. She shut down her website, suspended her Twitter account, and has disappeared from sight so effectively that she seems to have vaporized.

The commentary about all this was exceedingly vicious—the familiar stink of an online lynching, replete with the usual gleeful malice. Another overambitious writer reaching for the stars, then crashing to earth amidst the jeers of the crowd. Spiderbaby's lifted material included some sentences of mine, my informant—someone previously unknown to me—wrote. He seemed to expect a show of outrage, but I confess I was flattered. It was validation, a sign I'd made it, a tiny shot of love from the world. Though hardly enough of one—I found myself wishing I could have been plagiarized by someone a little higher up the literary food chain. I bet Leon Wieseltier attracts a better class of plagiarists.

When *is* enough ever enough when it comes to these bottomless wells of yearning for love and recognition? The fantasy of success isn't just about the concrete rewards—fame, money, sexual opportunities, and so on. No, it's the fantasy of an existential cure-all: an end to painful doubts about your self-worth, a massive fuck-you to everyone who ever dissed or doubted you, the assurance of your parents' undivided love.

Sure, I worry my ambitions are excessive, though I suspect that ambition is excessive by its very nature, predicated as it is on desire, which is calamitously inexhaustible too. I suppose it's why I'm still dwelling on James Frey's little ruckus these many years later: his excesses took a familiar shape. If I ever find myself on the receiving end of a national pillorying, no doubt it'll be over something I've published too. Until then, Frey is sort of my personal avatar, breaking the rules and taking the hits, while I watch from the bleachers. Maybe men have come to the end of their run, but they still have their uses, including as surrogate ids and superegos, waging big moral dramas on the world stage like action heroes trying to pummel each other to smithereens.

II

. . . . . .

NEUROTICS

The Victim

Rushdie had the Ayatollah, Job had God, and James Lasdun has Nasreen—or that's what he calls her in his memoir *Give Me Everything You Have*—the former creative-writing student who harassed him for five years, and at last word was apparently still at it. As Lasdun remarks mordantly, she made stalking into something of an art form.

Now, it's worth remarking, as regards this sort of protracted misery, that until fairly recently it's likely that no one but Lasdun's closest friends would have been privy to knowledge of it. But the New Man is no silent sufferer—recall Martin Amis's observation that the distinguishing feature of the type is a propensity for drawing attention to his wounds. Accordingly, no longer are today's male authors as inclined to sublimate their sufferings into the literary formulas associated with traditional masculinity, namely the Great American Novel. Increasing numbers are instead following emotive lady authors into the noisy wilds of the first-person confessional. "I always used to feel sorry for myself, having suffered four debilitating episodes of clinical depression and many years of moderate-to-severe dysthymia," is the way one male author recently opened his review of another male author's memoir about his chronic anxiety. Even if it was Rousseau who got the whole thing off the ground originally, and some classic bad-childhood memoirs by men are landmarks of the genre, it's tended to be a female-dominated form. Confessionalism had social urgency for women, especially when it came to matters conventionally screened from public view—incest and other childhood abuses, addictions, mental health glitches. . . . Writing a memoir was a way of refusing to be shamed about shame-ridden topics, which lent an aura of bravery to the enterprise, or did for its earlier practitioners.

Then everyone wanted to get on the bandwagon, to the point that memoirs began vying with the novel for literary cultural dominance, and may well have nosed ahead, in sales at least. But even if it's widely suspected (or muttered) that rampant narcissism more than bravery now fuels this sort of thing, luckily there's a corresponding rampant voyeurism about other people's private pain on the part of the reading public, who can't seem to get their fill of real-life miseries and foibles.

With male writers increasingly swept up in the confessional momentum, at least we're getting a less mythical vantage on men's inner lives, and closer-to-the-gut material than the familiar Successful Guy musings about careers well played and lives fully led. There's more vulnerability on view: anxiety and depression, divorce and destitution, urinary and other embarrassing conditions—the sorts of afflictions and woes that were once the hallmark of women's memoirs. It turns out that women have no monopoly on even classically "female" ailments: men have eating disorders too, men have trouble "down there," and now comes news that men too get sexually harassed, sometimes for years on end.

If there were a Harasser of the Year award it would have to go to Nasreen, a student in a graduate fiction-writing class that Lasdun, the English-born author of several exquisitely strange books of fiction and poetry, taught in New York in 2003—like many midlist authors, he's also an itinerant creative-writing professor on the side. Then in her early thirties, Nasreen had fled Iran for the US with her family during the revolution, which provided the setting for an ambitious novel-in-progress. She'd been polite and self-contained in class, meaning Lasdun learned only a few minimal facts about her at the time: she had a fiancé, she was a Muslim, she had talent. Two years later she emails him out of the blue, asking him to read a new draft of work he'd previously praised; he begs off by offering to put her in touch with his agent.

They start corresponding anyway—at first it's just chatty, soon a little flirtatious. Living a secluded country life upstate at the time, Lasdun admits that though he's happily married he doesn't mind being flirted with. Writers *are* especially prone to email flirtations, in my experience. There you are, sequestered at your keyboard hour after desperate hour, trying futilely to harness the vagaries of mental life into the discipline of prose, and email flirting is a far less taxing, though not entirely dissimilar, enterprise. At least it provides someone other than your own inner critic to commune with. In this case, Lasdun feels some actual affinity with Nasreen: they're on the same wavelength, he thinks; he genuinely admires her writing. Except that soon her emails are flooding his inbox, followed by pictures, then flirtation escalates into propositions—she offers to smuggle herself aboard a cross-country train trip he'll shortly be taking and constructs suggestive reveries about what they might get up to together on board. Alarmed, he reminds her that he's married, telling her bluntly that he doesn't want to be a figment in anyone's fantasies. In other words, he does and says all the correct things.

But once on the train he finds himself fantasizing about her too. "A sexual overture, however firmly resisted, is registered in a part of the psyche that has no interest at all in propriety or fidelity. . . . If the person making the overture is attractive and interesting, then that part of the psyche regards it as a matter of course that you will go ahead and sleep with them, and in fact regards it as a deeply unnatural act to choose not to." Lasdun's wonderfully frank on the hairy business of possessing a libido: the sad truth is that you and it are never entirely on the same team, are you? A libido is *not* an entirely trustworthy partner on one's journey through life. There you are, innocently going about your business, buying stamps or meeting with students, and some scene of astonishing perversity proposes itself to your brain as if out of nowhere, as though you weren't really as upstanding and circumspect as you know yourself to be. So when Nasreen's emails take a sudden ugly turn—"You fucking faggot coward, say something!" she demands in the face of Lasdun's newly cautious silence—however blameless he is in reality, having been a teensy bit roused by her provocations makes him feel, at some not entirely rational level, a teensy bit complicit in them. "When an attractive person makes you an offer like this, she or he establishes a powerful link to your own psyche, and whether or not you are interested in pursuing it, a whole new world of erotic possibility has become . . . latently present in your imagination," he rationalizes.

Then the accusations start escalating: He's ripping off her life for his work, he's guilty of emotional rape, racism, sexually exploiting students, and worse. Middle Eastern politics becomes a motif, which devolves into anti-Semitic insults and Holocaust gibes: "I think the holocaust was fucking funny. . . ." "Look, muslims are not like their Jewish counterparts, who quietly got gassed and then cashed in on it." "Your family is dead you ugly JEW." The ongoing hate mail is "like swallowing a cup of poison every morning, with usually a few more cupfuls to follow later in the day"—just one of the many arresting sentences Lasdun manages to wrench from this increasingly ugly situation. When Nasreen takes to smearing him all over the Internet and writing accusation-laden letters to the schools that employ him, he realizes he should start worrying about his reputation. If he doesn't get hired to teach a course, how will he know whether it was Nasreen's hate campaign that did him in with a would-be employer? He can't exactly *ask*.

But the unease goes deeper. Maybe it's because having an unseen tormentor is so close to the equivocal world of dream-life, where you're always guilty of some prior crime you can't remember having committed. And Nasreen is nothing if not psy-chologically shrewd: she has an uncanny way of intuiting his neuroses and insecurities, of getting under his skin; she reads him like a hostile psychoanalyst. Or maybe like a character from one of his own books—as a dedicated stalker she's obviously also an ardent student of his work, which gives her a leg up at penetrat-ing his defenses. Literary criticism is a paranoid endeavor in the best of cases: critics are always looking for what's beneath the surface, finding hidden patterns and connections that no one else sees. Nasreen's special talents in this area equip her to become Lasdun's very best reader. Plumbing his publications for buried messages and truths, eventually she knows his work better than he does, proposing subtle interpretations he can't help being intrigued by. I think most writers would acknowledge that there's some-thing about being astutely read that's kind of erotic—someone who reads you shrewdly has already burrowed rather deeply into your being, penetrated your social armor. It's happened to me occasionally: someone says something you hadn't thought of about

your work and you suddenly feel an unaccountable little ...
spark.

What makes this turn of events all the more uncanny for Lasdun is that a decade earlier he'd written a dark campus novel,
The Horned Man, with motifs strikingly similar to the situation
in which he now finds himself. The upright Lawrence Miller—a
gender-studies instructor, no less—is being hounded by a malev-
olent émigré disgraced former professor named Trumilcik, and
possibly framed for a series of sex crimes. Except that Lawrence
is not what you'd call a reliable narrator. He moves through life
in a dreamy fashion while people project things onto him, develop
elaborate hatreds, and engineer sabotage. Or so he reports. Bad
things just keep befalling him, out of nowhere. But is this Trumilcik even real? Or is he the rectitude-obsessed professor's alter
ego—the return of the repressed? "How I had managed to lay
myself open to an act of such preposterously elaborate vindic-
tiveness," the hapless Lawrence wonders—"with a pertinence I
struggle to find coincidental," adds Lasdun now, driven by subsequent real-life events to plumb his own backlist for portents. It's
as though he and his protagonist had changed places—or even
more peculiarly, as though the authorial unconscious can engineer the future.

A sly Freudianism sluices through Lasdun's oeuvre: fantasy
and reality aren't nearly as separable as the rational person would
prefer. People who pride themselves on virtue keep ending up
mysteriously sullied, in ways that mirror their desires and ambivalences. In his story "Cleanness," a son, decked out in rented
formalwear, drives to his father's wedding to a much younger
woman. After a series of wrong turns on unfamiliar country roads
and other mishaps, he arrives to find he's missed the nuptials.
He's also—accidentally? inevitably?—covered in sewage. No
matter: his disturbingly attractive new stepmother clasps the shit-

covered stepson to her frilly bosom anyway. The Oedipal and the excremental: what fertile turf Lasdun makes of them! Shit just happens, as in *The Horned Man*, when Lawrence, having benevolently left money in his office for Trumilcik, who may be camping there at night, returns to find the bills replaced by a coiled turd. Amateur Freudians will be cackling at the inside joke: money = shit in psychoanalytic symbology. (Anal types wish to retain both—yes, the relation between spending and toilet training is something all of us need to ponder thoroughly.)

The theme of exchanges and equivalences sets the Nasreen story in motion too: Lasdun offers career help; in return Nasreen shits all over him and plants fart jokes on his Wikipedia page. You can't help noticing that Lasdun's antic real-life tormentor seems cut from similar cloth as the id-like Trumilcik; that the atmosphere of ontological guilt *The Horned Man* summons echoes the self-interrogations of *Give Me Everything*. Is it fair to say that Lasdun authored both these foes? They certainly inhabit the same aesthetic universe, cronies in gleeful malevolence.

If Lasdun cuts Nasreen to suit his aesthetic temperament, it goes both ways. Nasreen generates a running commentary on her tactics, as if stalking were a form of performance art and she's an innovator in the field. She gets overly entranced with her role as an email terrorist, fancying herself as some kind of voice for the downtrodden. Though Lasdun doesn't mention her, she brings to mind Andy Warhol's would-be assassin, Valerie Solanas, whose *SCUM Manifesto* was equally crazed and paranoid, though with flashes of brilliant insight. (SCUM stood for Society for Cutting up Men, though it was a society of one.) Lasdun too can't help acknowledging the aesthetic dimensions of Nasreen's mischief-making exuberance: each of them is creating the other, he reflects; some Gothic transposition of consciousness has occurred.

Improbable though it sounds, she becomes a kind of muse.

Even though the ordeal turns him into a depressed, sleepless monomaniac, he's able to finish a story he'd been stalled on for a decade, finally understanding the desperation of a female character whose motives had eluded him. Eventually, of course, it occurs to him that a great trove of material had fallen into his lap, with Nasreen's malign intelligence releasing the creative energy in him to fuel a book. One of the pleasures of reading the results is how deeply we're embedded in the mucky war zone of the writer's imagination, spying on him while he grapples with his bizarre misfortune, and with Nasreen herself, finally wrestling the narrative away from her and remolding it into his own.

I did find myself wondering, in a practical-minded way, if it would have been wiser to just stop reading the horrible emails. Surprisingly, it's Lasdun's wife (mentioned only passingly) who advises him not to break off the correspondence with Nasreen, worried about inflaming her further. Then a police detective tells him he *has* to keep reading them in case there are actual—that is, legally actionable—threats. Though once there are actual threats no one's willing to do anything anyway—what you learn here is that law enforcement has no means of dealing with this sort of thing, thus prefers to ignore it. When Lasdun's local police department finally agrees to warn Nasreen by phone to lay off (by this point she's living in another state), she's imperiously unfazed.

In the meantime, Lasdun's growing more and more obsessed with his situation, turning himself inside out to decide what level of responsibility he bears for it. He feels unclean, living in the midst of Nasreen's onslaughts of hatred, yet can't stop thinking about her or talking about the situation to anyone who'll listen. He realizes he's becoming a bore, but then people with idées fixes invariably are.

But I sympathize with the obsessionality. Most of us who've taught for any length of time have had the occasional unhinged student, with various forms of unpleasantness ensuing. I myself was once targeted by such a student, and though the worst it ever got was incessant hang-up phone calls, it *was* weirdly preoccupying: I felt like I was being singled out by some unseen malignant force, like someone had it in for me in some personal way. Which turned out to be the case, though in fact I wasn't the true obsessional object: it was my ex-boyfriend, another professor in the same department. We'd only recently broken up after a long stormy entanglement, and I was in an unmoored state as it was (news alert: if you break up with someone you work with, daily painful reminders of his existence will become the substance of your workday). Then here comes this crazy former student of his, also apparently unmoored by him, who'd started calling both of us day and night and hanging up. Except that I didn't know it was a crazy student until, fed up with the hang-ups, I put the wheels of telephonic justice in motion, launching an investigation.

Unfortunately this ended badly for the student, whom I'll call Sharna, because a number of the hang-ups turned out to be coming, weirdly, from the state attorney general's office. I had a flash of Kafkaesque paranoia—what did they want with me? What did they know? When I finally contacted them, with no little indignation, the calls were tracked to Sharna, who'd been employed there doing something clerical after graduating, and was soon out of a job. When I learned her name and the other number she'd been calling, I of course contacted my ex, which I'd been desperately wanting to do for weeks. He was curt, saying he'd assumed the hang-up calls had been from me. I did learn an interesting fact from him, which was that Sharna had been in a couple of his classes, and they'd gone out for coffee once after she graduated. He insisted that was all there was, though allowed that maybe she'd had a bit of a crush on him. I had no idea how she knew about us in the first place as we'd tried to keep our thing a secret (including from our colleagues), but I suppose girls with crushes have special powers of observation. I did briefly wonder if anything else had happened between them, but by then at least the hang-ups had ceased.

However, it didn't end there, because Sharna's parents, who lived locally, contacted me via the department chair: they wanted us all to sit down and talk about the situation because, her father said, it may not have been Sharna who was responsible for the calls after all, there may have been "other forces" at work. The parents, who were not American-born and not exactly on the cutting edge of all the baffling new technologies (though neither was I—I didn't even have caller ID until all this started), were convinced that my ex had made the hang-up calls to me himself and had been able to make them appear to be coming from Sharna's phone. Nowadays this is apparently easy to do—in fact Nasreen was able to call Lasdun and make it look as though the calls were coming from elsewhere, but this was earlier on in the telephonic revolution and even caller ID was far from ubiquitous, which was probably why Sharna thought she could go undetected (if she'd thought about it at all).

The supreme irony of the situation was that I would have liked nothing more than to find out that the hang-ups were indeed coming from my ex—I suspect I'd half-hoped to find out this was the case when I acquired the fateful caller ID box. As I sat in the pleasant suburban living room while Sharna's father explained—in a scene Lasdun himself might have written—that my ex had fooled us all with his cleverly rigged caller ID override box, I deeply wanted to believe that it was true, that he wasn't over me either, and this was his roundabout way of letting me know. It was almost as though Sharna had intuited my innermost desires and engineered this little drama for her own perverse entertainment. I've half-believed ever since that when you become a figure in someone's disproportionate fantasies—even a bit player—the force field of their craziness gives them access to parts of your being you'd assumed were safely shielded from entry; and these interlopers, once installed, can be difficult to expunge.

And had my ex led Sharna on? *Had* there been more than coffee? So too Lasdun—had he done something to inflame Nasreen's imagination? Was there a meaningful glance, a double entendre, some inadvertent signal that might have made it seem they were meant to be each other's destinies? I never learned what Sharna hoped to accomplish with her hang-up calls since she never admitted to making them, though I do know that my ex was terminally seductive. After we split up, three different friends told me he'd come on to them, though I never really believed them. Obviously they'd misread the signals.

Lasdun is more self-conscious than my ex about his possible complicity, yet still baffled about what might have set Nasreen off. He doesn't like thinking that she was just mentally unbalanced as it would make her more generic, thus less interesting to write about. An unhelpful police detective he's put in touch with calls her a borderline personality—able to act crazy but control herself when necessary—but what do mental health labels accomplish? They come and go according to terminological fashion. Lasdun keeps thinking back to early on in their correspondence, when it still seemed like a harmless email flirtation, and to the time he and Nasreen had met for coffee—he'd finally agreed to read part of her manuscript and she wanted to give him the pages. In person she was an entirely different creature than the loquacious emailer: strangely absent, he later thinks. There'd been a chaste kiss-on-the-cheek parting.

Had Nasreen somehow become a different person than the one he'd met? Or was she someone other than he'd thought all along? Or a different person on the page than in person? We'll never know, and the ending to the story we want to read is precisely the one that can't be written, which is what happens when Nasreen herself reads the published book.

Are chaste kisses on the cheek between teachers and students erotic provocations? Had there been a kiss-on-the-cheek parting between my ex and Sharna? Is it possible to sufficiently eradicate erotic leakiness between teachers and students, such that misfired or misperceived signals become a thing of the past? It's generally understood that male professors are the ones more prone to such leakiness, though I personally know more than a few exceptions among the female professoriate. But Lasdun's not wrong when he reflects acerbically that in today's harassment-attuned culture, men occupy a place in society not unlike that of women in traditional societies: one whiff of sexual scandal can mean death. "Like them, our reputations were frail, in need of vigilant protection. We needed our own form of purdah, it seemed to me, our own yashmaks and chadors."

Nevertheless, he's contemptuous about the well-meaning sensitivity workshops they shuttle us professors to, and the increasingly restrictive campus codes that instill "paranoid extremes of self-monitoring." Of course, everyone who's not a sexual idiot knows that the price of employment in academia these days is that these wayward libidos of ours have to be throttled into obedience. But I suspect that even extremes of self-monitoring won't prevent professors from sparking the occasional imaginative chord in a student—and sometimes excessively imaginative ones.

What sets Lasdun's account of his experience apart is that as much as Nasreen's hate campaign derailed him, he's too exquisitely attuned to the daily difficulties of libidinal self-management—his own as well as his students'—to entirely pardon himself for it either. He's also uncomfortably aware of the extent to which the two of them came to mirror one another. "Her obsession with me achieved perfect symmetry: I became just as obsessed with her."

If there's a moral to this grim little story, it's that acting out prohibited desires isn't the only way to cause mayhem: regard the rancid turns that *not* acting on them can sometimes take. Lasdun's misfortune was to encounter someone whose obsessions he fired, and who refused to let him off the hook for not following through on what he thinks he never implied.

The Lothario

Via the grapevine I hear some startling news. Humorist Patricia Marx's oddly titled new novel, *Him Her Him Again the End of Him,* is apparently a roman à clef about an ex-boyfriend of hers, who happens to be someone I myself dated at one time too. Life is long and the world is small, so it stands to reason that you will occasionally encounter an ex turning up as a thinly disguised character in another of his previous girlfriends' satiric novels, but I feel a momentary rush of annoyance anyway. Dammit, why didn't I think of this first? He would have made such great material! I could have really skewered him! Then I remember that I'm not a novelist, nor a memoirist, and when I enter the ex's name in my carefully cultivated internal database of animus toward men, the hostility meter barely flutters. Still, you can probably understand why I was most eager to get my hands on an advance copy of this book.

A swirl of pre-publication rumor also leads me to believe that the ex gets quite a working-over from Marx. He was indeed something of a Lothario. Although short, he got around quite a bit, at least among a certain type of woman—the type I'm likely to encounter socially, it appears, as I keep running into other women who were also involved with him at some point, though thankfully none of us overlapped, which could prove awkward. But I was well aware that he cast a wide net: I recall mentioning his name once to my then hairstylist and even he knew someone who'd previously gone out with the man.

With this material, I figured Marx—a former writer for *Saturday Night Live*—could do a lot. The first woman elected to the *Harvard Lampoon,* she now writes occasional comic pieces for the *New Yorker,* meaning that she's been certified by various arbiters of American humor as "a funny woman." This is an exceedingly rare genus, at least according to a notorious throw-down by the late Christopher Hitchens in a 2007 issue of *Vanity Fair* titled "Why Women Aren't Funny." When it comes to sexual politics, Hitchens liked to get the ladies hoppin'. His argument is that men are simply more motivated than women to be funny since men want sex from women, whereas we females can get it anytime, on demand. And if a guy can get a girl to laugh—real open-mouthed, teeth-exposed, "involuntary, full and deep-throated mirth . . . well then, you have at least caused her to loosen up and to change her expression." (You know what he means: *deep-throated.*) Women also aren't funny because women are the ones who have to bear the children, these children might die, and you can't really make jokes about that.

Now, this is a fascinating portrait of female nature and relations between the sexes, though it's unclear which decade he had in mind: it has the slightly musty air of 1960-ish Kingsley Amis, wrapped in nostalgia for the merry days when sexual conquest required an arsenal of tactics deployed by bon-vivantish cads on girdled, girlish sexual holdouts. *"Oh, Mr. Hitchens!"* you imagine one of the potential conquests squealing at an errant hand on nylon-clad knee.*

As if to set Hitchens straight on what women really go for in a man, the unnamed heroine of Marx's novel—unnamed because it's written in the first person, meaning you have to keep pinching yourself to avoid falling into the biographical fallacy—is pathetically eager to have sex whenever possible with a man possessing absolutely no sense of humor whatsoever. The titular "him" is Eugene Lobello, a philosopher and academic Lothario who relieves the inexperienced protagonist of her unwanted virginity at the advanced age of twenty-one, while both are postgraduates at Cambridge. Not only is Eugene the furthest thing from funny there is, he's also utterly charmless, except, inexplicably, to the insecure and constantly self-deprecating heroine. Her friends all think he's a pretentious twit who's jerking her around, but having bestowed the gift of her virginity on him, she's apparently able to forgive him any form of churlish behavior. All she really wants is for the purportedly brilliant and infinitely narcissistic Eugene to think she's smart, thus she specializes in the erudite quip, a source of some of the book's funnier moments. On William Empson: "Don't you think a better title would be *Seven or Eight Types of Ambiguity?*"

There's nothing more alluring for many of us independent women than an unavailable boyfriend, and Eugene plays the role to the hilt, not least when he dumps the heroine to marry

---

* I should interject that despite my having published a few rather mocking remarks at his expense on this subject in *Slate,* where he had a regular column, Hitchens was kind enough to blurb my last book, always the mark of a gentleman in my view. Because it was my habit to pick arguments with him whenever I saw him over the years, to mask my ambivalent admiration among other reasons ("other reasons" would include most of his political positions, which admittedly did nothing to mitigate the intellectual crush), I fear that he never actually saw me at my funniest, which made me take the *Vanity Fair* piece all the more personally.

and impregnate the annoying and sniffly Margaret. (Quips our abandoned protagonist: "Hypochondriacs make me sick.") Her creative solution to Eugene's romantic flight is to rent the apartment directly above the newlyweds, where she can smell the curry odors wafting up from the dinner parties they don't invite her to. Marx is adept at sending up the familiar terrain of Women Who Love Too Much—you'd definitely like to get this girl on Dr. Phil for one of his tough-talking butt-kickings. But the fact that the humor usually ends up being far more at the heroine's expense than at Eugene's creates a more curdled than comic feeling. Eugene may be the ostensible target—saddled with cringe-inducing lines like "Your kisses are so recondite, my peach, that they are almost notional"—but she's the one who so relentlessly *loves* such a buffoon.

It's also disconcerting that these characters live in such different comedic universes: he's cartoonish, obtuse as an Oxbridge Homer Simpson, while her self-reflections have the ring of real human pondering and pain. Let me qualify that: real *female* human pondering and pain. It's not that men don't sometimes conduct themselves in a pathetic fashion when it comes to romance, but when they do they're "acting like little girls," in the current idiom—romantic dippiness is popularly coded as female. The heroine isn't unaware that Eugene doesn't love her, and that arguing and pleading and phoning a lot is a good way to "make someone who was hitherto lukewarm really detest you." Unfortunately, the less he loves her, the more convinced she becomes that "he and I could have been just the thing."

And remains convinced, against all odds. Seven years later, Eugene turns up in New York, where our still terminally insecure narrator now resides, having landed and been fired from a number of jobs (including one as a writer on a *Saturday Night Live*-like TV show called *Taped But Proud*), and she readily takes up with him once again. Eugene is in training to become a psycho-analyst (as a philosopher, he'd specialized in "ego studies," *ha ha*), and, though still married to Margaret, he lures the heroine into an affair that drags on for years. As a shrink, he's no more reliable than as a boyfriend: his pillow talk consists of divulging all his patients' secrets, and in the end it turns out he's been sleeping with one of his more attractive analysands, for whom he—yet again!—summarily dumps the heroine.

If there's humor to be milked from the common but wretched plight of loving someone who doesn't love you back, or from the variety of self-abnegating female behavior on display here, let's call it the humor of painful recognition. To the extent that it's funny, the comedy hinges on our willingness to recognize the element of truth in the parody. It struck me, while reading Marx's book, that the humor of painful recognition is an inherently conservative social form, especially when it comes to conventional gender behaviors, because it just further hardens such behaviors into "the way things are." The laughter depends on our recognizing the world as it is, and leaving it the way we found it. Like all cathartic laughter, it questions nothing. (This was Brecht's objection to catharsis in theater, which leaves audiences complacent and sheeplike; expelling our emotions instead of reflecting on what caused them.) By contrast, consider the comic sensibility of someone like Sarah Silverman. At her best, Silverman's scalding humor, delivered in that faux-naïf girly voice, leaves exactly nothing the same. When she takes on female abjection—most famously, "I was raped by a doctor. Which is so bittersweet for a Jewish girl"—clichés are defamiliarized and demolished; the world as it was is turned on its ear. The laughter isn't the laughter of painful recognition, it's the shock of sledgehammering feminine shame and smearing menstrual blood all over its covenants, not deferring to them with a chuckle.

Whether or not Hitchens was right and women are inherently less funny than men (he allowed that fat women, Jewish women, and lesbians are the exceptions—THANKS for that), women *are* highly funny when it comes to finely honed observations about the romantic and horizontal conduct of men, and it's on this terrain that Marx is a particularly keen observer. Though I was disappointed to recognize only a few superficial similarities between my own ex and Eugene, my antennae perked up when I came to a small moment between Eugene and the heroine, after he reenters her life. All that happens is this: the two of them are on the couch; he looks at her intently, makes a beckoning gesture with his forefinger, and says, "Come here."

That did have an awfully familiar ring. Back when I was on the receiving end of the move, I remember thinking that it seemed a bit Cary Grant–ish, but it never occurred to me that I was getting recycled material. I also didn't realize how comical it was until I read it reprised by Marx, though I felt a little unkind for thinking so. Like I said, I don't really have anything against this particular ex who, despite his own array of temperamental complications (including a monumentally crazy mother looming in the background), moved through the world with a certain courtliness and liked to whip up elaborate multi-course dinners for two. He would soon after embark on the tried-and-true second act of middle-aged male professors everywhere: marry a graduate student and have another child. It's like Botox for men apparently—though he was always preternaturally youthful-looking, when I ran into him recently he looked ten years younger than he had when I'd last seen him a decade before. Is this humor-worthy? Maybe if I envied him the opportunity to marry a graduate student and acquire a late-in-life offspring I'd be more inclined to lampoon his new life, but having taken a thorough self-inventory of all my currently unmet and/or impossible desires, I find that happily this isn't one of them.

On reflection, I'd append to Marx's mockery of our ex the qualifier that if our most intimate moments turn out to be pre-scripted, well obviously these are anxious encounters: failure hovers, rejection looms. No doubt there's a small buffer of added security in playing a role, or relying on what worked last time around. As Nick Carraway remarks of Gatsby, personality is an unbroken series of successful gestures; though maybe he should have added that the most successful gestures have been rehearsed in advance. But it's also more complicated than that. If you believe Freud, emotional life itself is all recycled material: no new disappointments, only old ones revived; no new attractions, only those earliest loves and hates imprinting every subsequent desire forever after.

It's easy enough to see why men might rankle and disappoint in the romantic sphere: bad copies of lost originals—even the best specimens would have to register as inept frauds, at least in the darker recesses of female emotional life. It's from these same recesses that jokes too originate, says Freud. I wonder if mocking male seduction techniques is such a comedic gold mine for this reason, because jokes and disappointment share the same home base.

Now that men have become less economically necessary and there's less reason than ever to pretend to admire them, scorn for men has become the postfeminist fallback position, widely regarded as a badge of feistiness and independence. Nevertheless, men remain conduits to things a lot of women still deeply want: sex, love, babies, commitments. . . . It's a contradictory situation to find oneself in, to say the least. And not really *that* funny, but get a bunch of women in a room, add liquor, and jokes about men's inadequacies fly like shrapnel. When it comes to dating, single men are dogs, infants, sex-obsessed, moral rodents, or emotional incompetents. And once you finally land one, nothing much improves, since husbands are morons, selfish, workaholics, emotionally unavailable, and domestically incompetent. Single men lie and mislead to get sex; husbands have lost interest in sex entirely. Men are emotionally autistic, except for all the ones who want you to be their mother. Men can't talk about their feelings! Except for all the ones who won't shut up about themselves. They're macho assholes, except when they're wimps—what man could endure childbirth? And so on.

In *Women on Men*, Liza Donnelly, a *New Yorker* cartoonist—thus, along with Marx, another officially certified funny woman—makes the case for ridiculing men as a form of female assertion. In a running commentary about her assembled cartoons she suggests, as potential comedic material, men's misplaced egos, bravado, hot air, childish behavior, self-obsession—their other obsessions include sports, cars, and gadgets—and, of course, their preoccupation with sex, one of her frequent cartoon subjects. (A woman speaking about her husband: "His body is fifty, his mind is thirty, and his penis is thirteen." Another woman ordering in a restaurant, speaking of her date: "I'd like a Chardonnay, and I'm fairly certain he'd like sex.") The goal, says Donnelly, is to "Make them uncomfortable. Make them squirm. Because we love them." One notices that this is love mixed with a healthy dose of aggression. (A man and a woman are ordering in a restaurant; the woman says to the waiter: "What wine do you recommend I throw in his face?" Another man and woman are in a car; the woman says to the gas station attendant: "Forget the windshield. Please just wipe the silly smirk off his face.")

Donnelly offers a few telling glimpses into how her own life has fueled her humor; interestingly, her dating career seems to have echoed that of Marx's heroine. Donnelly too kept being drawn to men who weren't available—not willing to settle down, not wanting to leave their wives. . . . "You name it, I fell for them all." For a long time she thought marriage wasn't for her and married people were aliens, though at some point she realized that all men have their "side effects" (like medicine?), and the real question is which side effects you can tolerate. Her story ends relatively happily: she marries a fellow cartoonist who provides her with plenty of male foibles to humorize about. All in all a good match, except that he doesn't dance. And is a little sex-obsessed. And some other stuff.

Are ambivalent women funnier? This is a category Hitchens neglected to include on his exceptions list, but I'd like to think so. I'm hardly in a position to suggest that women shouldn't be ambivalent about commitment, because everyone should be, in my opinion—note that the same term covers stints in a mental asylum. And if women who are ambivalent about commitment are drawn with suspicious frequency to men who are unattainable, far be it from me to begrudge anyone the consolations of venting about men's immaturity and egotism in response. After all, it's not like getting stuck with the guy and waking up to the same mug day after day is without its ambivalences either, as Donnelly's cartoons attest. A woman to her girlfriend: "I always saw marriage as a stepping-stone to divorce." A woman to her date: "I love the idea of you, but not you." Another woman to another date: "You are exactly the kind of guy I could learn to leave." A woman about her inert husband: "Nobody told me marriage would be an endurance test."

For funny women, each man is his own unique recipe for disappointment. From their laundry lists of male failings it can be tempting to deduce that women humorists specialize in wanting what men don't have to give, or perhaps in wanting from each particular man the particular thing he's most unable to provide, whether it's an account of his feelings, a respite from ESPN, or lifelong fidelity. And when men *do* come through, look for an ulterior motive: Donnelly says that men who cook for women are only doing it to prove they're good in bed, which caused me to re-evaluate my ex's culinary flair. Hmm, so *that's* what he was up to.

The term "misogyny" is often proffered to explain the historic male–female predicament, but it's not like women are so fond of men at the moment either. Researchers who study these things generally find far higher levels of rage among women toward men than among men toward women. Still, hope springs eternal— maybe the right man will come along soon. Maybe one who will commit! And not interrupt! And a lot of other stipulations. There's no reason that longing to merge with a man has to include either respecting or liking him, which is one of the more comedic aspects of heterosexual relations at present.

The question is whether this is an entirely good-faith enterprise. What I mean is: to the extent that jokes mask disappointed desires, aren't they just an index of your disavowed dependency on the very thing you're so busy scorning? The problem with scorning men isn't that it's unfair to them, it's that it makes them all the more emotionally central. To compound the problem, in these post-conventional times, men have fewer incentives than ever to deliver the goods, which exacerbates their capacity to disappoint, which maximizes their emotional centrality.

Still, it's a universally acknowledged truth that these errant and frustrating men could gratify female needs and desires if only they were somehow different than they are. Less like *men*, to begin with.

Humiliation Artists

Among the many sources of humiliation I either learned about or was forced to relive while reading Wayne Koestenbaum's *Humiliation*: having a tiny penis or any form of smallness, soiling oneself and other bodily inadvertencies, writing or being written about, being jealous, being cheated on, being Googled, being mistaken for the wrong gender, impotence, hair loss, inadvertent erections in awkward circumstances, disfigurement, smelling like liverwurst, vomiting onstage before a musical performance, and being photographed after you're dead. As we see, the list goes on indefinitely, with humiliation pursuing us from our earliest childhood memories well into the afterlife. As Koestenbaum, a cultural critic and poet, points out, we all live on the edge of humiliation all the time, "in danger of being deported to that unkind country." Being gay, he's especially interested in men's experience of humiliation, much of which comes wreathed in sexual shame.

As it happens, while I was reading *Humiliation*, another expert on male humiliation was demonstrating his own proficiency in the subject, this time on the national news. Though straight, this New

York congressman also chose sexual shame as his arena. He'd been exposed doing something exceedingly peculiar and, many felt, perverse—he didn't simply have an affair, as per the usual politician scandal; this was worse: he *hadn't* had an affair. Instead, he'd sent a lewd cell phone photo of himself to a twenty-one-year-old college student he'd never met, then committed the fatal error of lying about it to the press and his colleagues once the photo went public, as it inevitably would. When he finally admitted he'd sent the photo ("I'm deeply ashamed"), he refused to resign: he was going to take a leave of absence and undergo some sort of therapeutic regimen. Other embarrassing texts and even dirtier photos started surfacing. It soon emerged that he'd been exchanging raunchy texts, emails, and dirty pictures with at least six different women for over three years, *using his own name*. The fact that the name in question—Anthony Weiner—also happened to be a sexual pun escaped no one's notice.

What *is* the great attraction of humiliation for men, a question we're forced to grapple with when considering the regular parade of elected officials performing similarly imaginative acts of public self-immolation in recent years? Weiner was energetic enough at it to parlay a fairly minor offense into full-scale national disgrace. Consider his opening salvo after the story first broke: he couldn't "say with certitude" that the dirty pictures weren't of him. Congressmen who've had actual sex with actual prostitutes have escaped with barely a ripple in the news cycle compared with the public bloodbath Weiner engineered. The word "humiliation" became a steady drumbeat in the news reports: he'd humiliated his wife, he'd humiliated himself, he'd even humiliated Speaker of the House Nancy Pelosi.

As these events unfolded, a lot of people were saying knowingly that this was a story about how technology has changed the landscape of intimacy and fidelity; I believe this is known as "the

Internet made me do it." But I prefer Koestenbaum's route into the subject, by way of the literary imagination, to the reductive techno-determinism so popular among cultural pundits. People had problematic desires a long time before the Internet came along. Also, with electoral politics looking more and more like a form of public psychotherapy, one literary text in particular struck me as an especially useful guide to such matters: the decidedly pre-Internet *Portnoy's Complaint*, since where else but in a satirical novel about a nice Jewish boy and his libido would the crotch-obsessed analysand's name really be Weiner? Reading the hourly news updates on Weiner's story did feel like living inside a Philip Roth novel, with Speaker Pelosi standing in for the castrating Sophie Portnoy in a rollicking sequel to Roth's classic saga of sexual shame. They should have called the update Weiner's Complaint, instead of the too-obvious Weinergate—there was Pelosi threatening to chop off Weiner's career, and when no less an Oedipal figure than the president of the United States stepped in to say that if it were him, he'd resign, Weiner finally bowed to the inevitable. Taking the proffered dagger, he smote himself dead—politically dead anyway, which was what mattered.*

Personally, I thought he shouldn't have resigned from Congress, but I wasn't consulted. But rereading *Portnoy* I came upon something I'd forgotten: Roth's epigraph, in the form of a psychiatric journal extract, defining "Portnoy's Complaint" as a disorder "in which strongly-felt ethical and altruistic impulses are perpetually warring with extreme sexual longings, often of a perverse nature." This seemed apropos. Though unfortunately, the epigraph con-

---

* And how many centuries before they stop appending "gate" to every scandal anyway, which only caught on after Nixon loyalist–turned–columnist William Safire started doing it as a clever way of minimizing his former boss's crimes against the country, multiplying the "gates" ad infinitum to strip the original one of importance?

tinued, all this energetic exhibitionism and auto-eroticism can yield no gratification, only "overriding feelings of shame and the dread of retribution, particularly in the form of castration." Or such is the conclusion of Portnoy's psychoanalyst, one Dr. Spielvogel—the quote is from his scholarly article "The Puzzled Penis," for which Alexander Portnoy's sex life provided the case study material. By the way, Portnoy is *also* in government—he's the "Assistant Commissioner of Human Opportunity for the City of New York."

Human opportunity *indeed*. Isn't it the perpetual lure of such "opportunities" that keeps imploding people's careers and marriages? In the case of Weiner's Complaint, it's we the electorate, watching these implosions unfold in the headlines, who are tasked with reprising Dr. Spielvogel's role—in case you've forgotten, the whole book-length rant was addressed to Spielvogel, just as Weiner's Complaint is, arguably, to us. "Now vee may perhaps to begin. Yes?" is the sole thing the doctor says—one of those tight-lipped Freudians, you infer—in the book's mordant closing line.* And what would Spielvogel have made of Weiner's Complaint, had he managed to get the congressman on the couch? We'll have to proceed by inference—or, better yet, turn to the more voluble Dr. Koestenbaum for direction.

Though equally a student of shame, Koestenbaum is less interested in the motives for seeking humiliation than in an *ethics* of humiliation. He wants us, when witnessing spectacles like Weiner's Complaint, to refuse to shame the already shamed, even those who seem to be vigorously seeking it out; the ethical position in

---

* In fact, Roth's own psychoanalyst did make use of not very thinly disguised details of Roth's life in a published case study—this is Roth converting his own humiliation into fiction. He couldn't let it drop though, and brought Spielvogel back in *My Life as a Man,* where the analyst once again unapologetically rips off his patient's life for a journal article.

such cases is to minimize humiliation, not inflict it. "We're all in the business of cleansing ourselves of shame," he diagnoses, putting us on the couch along with the humiliation seekers. However skillful the provocation, he's determined not to participate. His brand of therapy involves forging allegiances instead: with sexually disgraced politicians or anyone with "a complicated sexual agenda." Presumably this would include the complicated Congressman Weiner, as even former senator Larry Craig, the long-standing gay-rights foe caught making solicitations in an airport bathroom, gets a reluctant sympathy vote from Koestenbaum. No one should be humiliated for sex, not even sexual hypocrites.

Of course where Koestenbaum has the advantage over Weiner, or sad sacks like Craig, is that writers get a lot more social leeway when it comes to expressing potentially humiliating proclivities than do politicians—gay, straight, or indeterminate. Indeed, not only has Koestenbaum devoted much of his career to exposing himself—his obsessions with opera divas, and Jackie O., and in *Humiliation*, his sexual fantasies about students—and shows no signs of stemming the flow of radical self-exposure, he hasn't been punished for these preoccupations, or forced to resign his position as a Distinguished Professor of English. In fact he's been steadily promoted. Unlike Weiner, he had the foresight to choose a line of work in harmony with his being.

Lacking the same self-acuity, Weiner chose the nonstop scrutiny of politics as his arena of achievement, consigning himself to what can only have been a painfully fractured existence. Yearning to express more dimensions of himself to someone—to anyone—grasping for sympathy and affirmation from the universe, he seized on the new communication technologies as an outlet. The digital gadgetry pervading our lives does offer all sorts of possibilities for creative perversity, opportunities many of us have indeed explored, with occasionally humiliating outcomes. (A word to the wise: the impulsive cell phone video you make with today's beloved is tomorrow's revenge porn.) But creativity and perversity have always been kissing cousins—Freud thought they have the same instinctual origins, by the way. Thus where others have stressed the icky perversity of Weiner's photographic pursuits, I'd like to take a different route, and consider their self-expressive dimensions instead.

Creative expression does often put unconscious elements into play; you invariably reveal more about yourself than you know or can control. Consider the photo of Weiner holding up a handwritten sign with an arrow pointing to himself, labeled "Me," sent to one of his online friends. I suppose he meant to be proving to the ostensible recipient that he was indeed who he'd claimed to be, an actual Congressman, though when I saw it my immediate thought was: It's like he's picking himself out of a lineup.

For what crime though? It was an uncanny image, prophetic of the exposure and shame to come. "This is who I *am*," it also seemed to say. The message was a dual one. Koestenbaum writes that humiliation has the structure of a fold; the inner and outer realms change place, as in folding a napkin, though another of his examples is more pertinent to our inquiries than a well-set table: "Think of a defendant, in a trial, seeing his or her underwear presented as evidence by the prosecutor. An object that should be private and unseen is suddenly visible." It's an apt way of describing Weiner's uncomfortably self-prosecutorial photographic style. Indeed, the first photo that surfaced *was* of his underwear—or, more precisely, of an erection thinly concealed behind gray boxer briefs.

Inner and outer realms changing places is also a good analogue for what tends to happen in the artistic process: interior life finds its way into some kind of exterior object or product. Reading this photo the way a critic or curator might, one would say its overriding aesthetic feature is the oscillation between concealment and exposure: the erection is apparent, but not fully visible; the body is exposed, but the face isn't. Who is this artist? Someone flirting with visibility? Someone for whom excitement is defined as risk-taking, who staged this performance for that reason? The photo *is* obviously taken by the person who's portrayed: he's the auteur—scriptwriter, stage manager, costume designer, star (in other words, every element is there by his design).

And the intended audience? It's evident the photo wasn't contrived for the recipient alone; there was a larger audience in mind, or the rest of us wouldn't be looking at it. Or let's say, in *some* corner of his mind. As befitting a man whose name is a sexual pun, the performance turns on a sort of pun too: he's exposing himself to *expose* himself. The humiliation didn't come after the fact—after the public outing, the hasty lies, the eventual mea culpa—it was there from the very beginning, it's written all over the photo. As with the erection itself—apparent, but not completely visible; like the famous purloined letter, hidden in plain sight. Note another bit of punning: being "caught with your pants down" isn't only an idiom, these photos tell us, it's literal too. It so recalls the awful dream of showing up at a dinner party (or giving a lecture or walking down the street) in your underwear—the variations are endless—but this time it's for real, in front of the entire world.

You have the underwear dreams too, right? I've been haunted by them as long as I can remember. Why can't we scrape these images out of our psyches? Koestenbaum recalls the indelible sight of a third-grade schoolmate, pants around his ankles, being paddled across his naked buttocks by the teacher as punishment for some infraction. The buttocks were pimply; girls could see the boy's penis. The queasy mixture of fascination, horror, and shame provides the model for every humiliation to come, Koestenbaum says, which is the reason he's come to think of humiliation as a contagion. When we're witnesses to other people being humiliated we share in it; we *catch* it. Even the teacher administering the paddling was humiliated; she'd abandoned her dignity, she'd "dragged the class into a turgid, low zone."

Would Koestenbaum say that's where Weiner dragged us too? But did we catch something from him, or did we propel ourselves into that low zone by playing eager witness to his public shaming? This is my question: what should our relationship be with people who arrange for us to catch them doing shameable things, especially if you think, as I can't help thinking, that Weiner sent that photo to *us;* the college student was just an intermediary. Or is this too unequivocal—is it kinder to say that he "accidentally" sent it to us; he "meant" to send it to the student and somehow pressed Send All instead? (This was Weiner's explanation for how the first photo went public—clumsy typing.) But why quibble over details: exposure was inevitable. He merely sped the process along, as though impatient for Judgment Day to arrive.

So in Koestenbaum's terms, Weiner humiliated us as well as himself, though Koestenbaum would probably add—with his usual mischievous perversity—that this kind of thing can be strangely exhilarating. And also unsettling. What I find myself wondering is whether Koestenbaum's mercilessly shamed third grader evolves into the defendant whose underwear incriminates him in court or the congressman flashing his crotch shots in public until the hammer of social punishment crashes down. Do the disciplinary horrors of childhood somehow transmute into the grotesque self-inflicted injuries of adulthood?

When the sex photos first surfaced, and Weiner was still maintaining that his Twitter account had been hacked, he tried brushing the whole thing off as a joke on his name. While denying that he was responsible for sending the photos, he was weirdly intent on linking his name to the mysterious hacker's purpose. Except there was nothing to suggest any connection. Nevertheless . . . On CNN he said, "When you're named Weiner, this happens a lot." "When you're named Weiner, it goes with the territory." By my count he mentioned his name five times in a four-minute interview. I couldn't help wondering what it was like growing up with that taunt-inspiring name—what sort of playground mockery was involved, what humiliations imprinted on his psyche.

So why set yourself up for a reprise of childhood humiliation—wasn't once enough? Here we enter murky territory. The experience of humiliation plays a larger role in sexuality than we like to think, says psychiatrist Robert Stoller, writing about what he calls "the theater of risk" in erotic life. What looks from the outside like risk-taking sexual behavior—exhibitionism is the example he gives—can be a way of transforming early humiliations into triumphs. The risk taker seeks out dangerous situations as a proving ground, to measure his success at avoiding a greater risk, humiliation. It's what's *concealed* that's the crucial missing piece of information: namely, the mark that humiliation has left on the person's erotic life. As in Weiner's photos, there's an aesthetics of the visible and the hidden. Needless to say, it's a treacherous strategy; the real-life consequences can be devastating. Weiner didn't convert humiliation into triumph; all he managed to do was relive it.

The more you nose around the subject of humiliation, the more perplexed you become about what pleasure actually *is*. To say that people don't always use sex exclusively for pleasurable purposes is a pretty vast understatement. Yet how much can we grasp about the alternative purposes? Those "caught with their pants down" aren't typically very forthcoming about what they hoped to accomplish. Weiner, once exposed, said, "I don't know what I was thinking," after he finally admitted sending the incriminating photos. "This was a destructive thing to do." He further non-elaborated, "If you're looking for some kind of deep explanation for it, I simply don't have one."

No doubt anyone in possession of a libido has experienced the

occasional fissure between brain and groin, and knows how carefully both must be monitored to avoid personal catastrophe. "I
don't know what I was thinking" is a phrase many of us have had
cause to utter on occasion. Alcohol, that great disinhibitor, is a
convenient after-the-fact explanation. Still, the general view is that
when the brain suspends operations, it's in the pursuit of enjoyment, not pain and humiliation. "I wasn't thinking" is the custom-
ary code for "I had to stop thinking to have some fun." The idea
that we're pleasure-seeking animals tragically constrained by the
encumbrances of civilization is a lot more palatable than the idea
that we're destruction-seeking animals pursuing opportunities to
degrade and humiliate ourselves in front of the world.

Koestenbaum's novel strategy is to do it deliberately instead of
inadvertently. Embrace your humiliation! Along with the hapless
Senator Craig, public bathrooms provide the settings for some of
his most memorable humiliations too—so we learn here—as he's
not just a theorizer of the subject, he's also performing it page by
page, offering his readers "some details about my own penis and
its proclivities" to amplify humiliation's universality. Take the time
he was snubbed by a catheterized wheelchair-bound man in a train
station men's room who, though positioned hopefully in front of
the urinals, was clearly waiting for someone sexier than the author
to arrive. Koestenbaum ups the ante by telling us that he snubbed
the wheelchair guy too—they were both waiting for someone sexier to arrive. He's not just a reject, he's an *ableist*, which in today's
climate is far more humiliating than just being an ordinary pervert.
    Spinning out such episodes for maximum possible embarrass-
ment is his show of solidarity with outcasts everywhere. As is
writing about them to begin with, since writing is deeply humiliating for him too. You're begging for a response that may not be

forthcoming, and unreciprocated desire is always humiliating. *Any* reader's dislike of your work is an injury: you've offered yourself to them, like offering your body to be caressed, and being refused is shaming. When he writes of editors rejecting commissioned essays and reviews ("a botch," one declares nastily), or a publishing-house acquaintance taking unseemly glee in having shot down a submitted manuscript, or books he'd warmly inscribed to a revered poet turning up at a used-book store—now he's tapping my own deepest reservoirs of shame. I find myself doing a quick mental inventory: has this happened to me? It's like checking your limbs after witnessing a car accident to reassure yourself that you're still intact.

Humiliation concludes with a numbered compendium of Koestenbaum's lifetime humiliations, from a disgustingly messy sneeze in fourth grade, up through more recent mortifications, like being told he has a flat ass. He may find writing humiliating, but he's also lucky enough to be excited by the creative dimensions of humiliation. And here's where I get off the bus—constructing a list of my favorite humiliated moments would be impossible for me, let alone publishing it. Even the thought makes me physically uncomfortable. Would I be a better writer if I cherished my humiliations more? I *don't* cherish them, even though I suspect that every accumulated wound and misery seeps out onto the page in every sentence you write. Writers are compelled to flash their underwear around in public too, camouflaged to varying degrees by form or craft, with critics playing the sadistic teachers, camouflaged to varying degrees by attacks on your form or craft. Yes, it's back to the third-grade classroom with every sentence you write, which is part of what makes it so excruciating. Sure, writing has its moments of sublimity—grasping after the ineffable, realizing something just out of reach—yet at every instance mod-

ulated by the chronic substratum of shame about having taken a
dump in public.

For Koestenbaum, writing *is* very much something you do
with your body. He makes the analogy explicit in an earlier
essay called "Darling's Prick," which opens with Darling, a character in Genet's *Our Lady of the Flowers,* tracing the contours
of his penis on a piece of paper and mailing it to his lover. For
Darling, the dotted line is shorthand for something that desperately needs to be expressed, something essential about himself—
call it a proto-selfie, if that makes it more intelligible. For
Koestenbaum, this gesture of Darling's is a metaphor for the
enterprise of writing itself, and the urgency he wants his own
writing to have.

Notice that Darling and Weiner share a certain aesthetic bent.
For Weiner too, there was something he needed to convey with
those photos that he didn't have another way of saying. If only
he'd been a character from Genet instead of a politician from
Queens! He may have used a cell phone in lieu of paper, but let's
imagine that he too was tracing the contours of something essential, however inchoately. "Assume there is a state of mind called
'wanting to say,'" Koestenbaum suggests about Darling and, I'd
imagine, about himself. From here, the humiliated congressman
and the writer struggling for words—or any human groping for
language—don't look like such different animals.

It used to be women who were the hysterical sex, their bodies
racked with sexual conflicts and emotional excesses. They were
endlessly photographed and sketched, mid-paroxysm; the medical establishment turned them into a sideshows—recall the famous
1887 painting of Freud's mentor Jean-Martin Charcot trotting out

his favorite hysteric, "Blanche," who cooperatively swoons before a packed seminar room of physicians at the Salpêtrière clinic.

By the end of the twentieth century, it was men who were racked by sexual conflict, dedicated to playing out their inner lives in public. And not in the political sphere alone: watching male bodies being thrashed became a constant in other corners of the culture too. Masculinity became entangled with punishment, or at least it was a major cinematic motif: men getting beaten to a pulp and asking for more, in movie after movie, like one unending Fight Club. Sometimes it's played for laughs—Mel Gibson is the emblematic late-twentieth-century figure here, ricocheting between clowning and crucifixion, on-screen and in life. But even when comedic, it's still painful to watch.

Are these tough guys showing how indestructible they are or penitents lined up for absolution? Or to put it another way: what *does* it mean to be a man clinging to power at this point in history?

In Jonathan Lethem's essay collection *The Disappointment Artist,* he writes about his obsession with John Ford's 1956 psychosexual epic *The Searchers*, featuring John Wayne's unsettling performance as the racist, enraged, and hysterical Ethan Edwards, out to avenge white men's losses in post–Civil War Texas. After spending years tracking down his young niece, abducted by Comanches, shockingly, Edwards tries to murder her when he finds her living as the wife of a Comanche leader. Lethem comes to realize—after watching the movie a dozen times, beginning as a college student in 1982—that it *speaks* to him in some complicated way: if Wayne (playing against type) is an icon for male neurosis, the film is putting Lethem's own neurotic symptoms under the microscope too. For him, the real subject of *The Searchers* is masculinity stretched to its breaking point.

But his obsession with the film is also humiliating: he's jeered and misunderstood by classmates and friends who can't see past the misogyny and racism, not to mention the outdated codes of manhood—Wayne's performance is so overwrought at times it's just this side of camp. Still, something in this convoluted film expresses his inner reality, Lethem comes to think.

Lethem's lucky—like Koestenbaum, he gets to use culture as a shopping mall of obsessions, a playing field for expressive perversity, to figure out what he doesn't understand about himself. Sure there are perils to writing your inner life's deepest story in public. (Koestenbaum enumerates his bad reviews in *Humiliation*, another thing I'd be too mortified to do.) But at least the two of them have the leeway to explore the darker depths of masculinity in all its incoherencies without enduring national disgrace.

Weiner went a different route. Two years after the first public humiliation, he attempted a political comeback, running for mayor of New York City, even briefly leading in the polls. *Very* briefly: new revelations soon emerged that he'd actually continued sexting various women even after he'd resigned from Congress, using the late-night comedy-ready pseudonym "Carlos Danger."

Credit must be given: if anyone's a true Humiliation Artist, it's Weiner. Stay tuned for the next comeback attempt.

The Manly Man

The big problem I had debating the eminent political philosopher Harvey Mansfield—neocon hero and William R. Kenan Jr. Professor of Government at Harvard—about his deeply offensive and deeply anxious book *Manliness* was that he was just so nice about it that it brought out the dominatrix in me. I wanted to bend him over a chair and thrash him black and blue with a riding crop. This isn't a fantasy I'm accustomed to entertaining, especially about seventy-five-year-old Harvard professors, but I swear he was asking for it.

I wasn't the only one who felt this way, as by that point Mansfield was being publicly flogged on a regular basis by an assortment of heavy hitters on the liberal left—it was like the book had a "Kick Me" sign on it. Martha Nussbaum had knocked him around in the *New Republic* for what she said was shoddy scholarship and illogic (according to an online commentator, she'd made him "her bitch"); Garry Wills had written a long, condescending takedown in the *New York Review of Books*, funnily titled "Mousiness." Nussbaum and Wills took *Manliness* very seriously as an expression of ideas about sexual politics: they mounted attacks on those ideas, they fumed about Mansfield's failure to be sufficiently enlightened about gender progress. But it wasn't entirely clear to me, once I met him, that Mansfield himself took his ideas that seriously: he meant them as a provocation, obviously; but also, I started to think, as flirtation.

His basic argument is that society needs manliness, which he defines in contradictory ways. At its best it's "confidence in the face of risk," though it can also be violent and stubborn. But we need manliness because all the great leaders and innovators throughout history have possessed it, Mansfield says, and feminism is trying to kill manliness off by promoting a gender-neutral society. Feminism is putting the future of humanity in peril! There are also a lot of summary statements about male and female nature along the way, such as that men are risk takers, whereas women shun risk and perceive it more readily than men—we fear spiders, for instance.

There are certain men who just like getting women mad at them, for reasons that are open to speculation. This is not always an endearing or benign trait: Mansfield was the sole faculty member at Harvard to vote against a women's studies program, which is certainly one way to get a lot of women mad at you. At least he practiced his own code: "Manliness loves, and loves too much, the position of being embattled and alone against the world." *

It's probably not a good thing about me when it comes to institutional politics, but I find it hard to get that worked up about dumb expressions of unreconstructed sexism. For one thing, in my experience it's the subtle forms that are most insidious (these are

---

* He was also a big supporter of former Harvard president Lawrence Summers, who became embroiled in controversy and eventually resigned after publicly questioning women's aptitude for science.

not practiced exclusively by men). Also I'm just lazy: I don't like having to rise to the bait like some sort of earnest marionette. It's too exhausting. I prefer to just spread a thick layer of irony over the situation and hope my opponents smother in it.

Mansfield and I ended up together onstage in this awkward intellectual blind date because we were both supposed to be contrarians about gender. I'd recently written a book about femininity and its discontents (*The Female Thing*); he was touting the manly virtues and trying to get feminists to take him on. The general argument of *The Female Thing* is that women are stuck ping-ponging between feminism and traditional femininity, which are incompatible ways of being in the world, which is why gender relations are messed up at the moment. Mansfield's book actually echoes some of the same themes, though unlike him I don't think there's an essential female nature that feminism tries to minimize and suppress. I just think we're living in transitional times. Someone had the bright idea of having us hash it out in front of an audience.

We met for the first time shortly before the event was scheduled to start. Though I'd been prepared to loathe him, Mansfield was so courtly and deferential that I found myself quite disarmed. I'd been asked to summarize the differences between our books, so after the moderator introduced us, I went first.

What follows are excerpts from an edited version of the conversation.

LAURA KIPNIS: I was planning on starting out on a conciliatory note and saying that I hated Harvey's book—can I call you Harvey?—far less than I thought I was going to, since I know from my close reading of *Manliness* that it's women's nature to be modest and conciliatory, and I'm doing my best to comply. Also I don't feel like playing the role of the upright feminist here and having to defend feminism against a lot of silly potshots, which I'd find boring and so would everyone else. That ground has been covered too many times already, and even Harvey concedes at the end of his book that there's no going back to traditional gender roles, and no recapturing some previous version of male privilege. Even he's willing to defend certain of feminism's achievements—

[*Mansfield starts to speak but I cut him off.*]

—you can correct me later if I'm wrong.

And, in fact, I found the first third of the book quite interesting—I thought I recognized a fellow contrarian. But I must say the kindred feeling came to an end when I got to your ideas about feminism which, frankly, verge on male hysteria. By hysteria, I mean that vast quantities of anxiety are being generated about a completely invented and artificial threat, namely your idea that what feminists want is to eliminate all differences between the sexes.

So I'd like to shift the focus instead to what I think is the book's *real* concern, which is: What happens between men and women in the private realm, once sexual equality is achieved? The anxiety is that feminists have tried to enforce what the book calls "gender neutrality."

[*to Mansfield*] You use this term a lot, and frankly, it's completely spurious! Gender neutrality isn't anyone's goal, and it's certainly not what's taken place! Walk down the street: Are men wearing skirts? Are men wearing lipstick? It's not as though gender differences have been eliminated, or are going to be anytime soon. Which is why I'm calling this an *anxiety* rather than an argument. It's a symptom of something that goes deeper. So I think we can take your concerns seriously as *symptoms*, even while agreeing that they have no actual basis in lived reality.

So having said that, let me try to briefly outline—

[*The audience laughs, as I've already been going on for some time.*]

—some of the areas of agreement and disagreement between our two books, and then you can take it from there, okay?

[*Mansfield is looking a little stunned by this barrage of words, but appears to agree.*]

Okay, so another of the big anxieties in your book is that feminists aren't any fun in bed.

[*More audience laughter.*]

And that feminist sexuality isn't erotic. You say that feminists have successfully eliminated differences between the sexes, and you believe that sex requires gender roles to make it hotter—okay, maybe you don't say it *precisely* this way, I'm paraphrasing.*

So I'd like to reassure you on all these counts. First, I don't even necessarily disagree with the idea that gender roles make sex hotter, and I suspect you'd find a lot of other feminists who wouldn't disagree. Which means, to start with, that you're simply mistaken when you collapse all feminists together and say that what we all want is equality in the bedroom. By the way, even a lot of same-sex couples still want to re-create traditional gender roles. So if a few gender-neutral couples out there are having bad sex, I feel like that's not something you can really blame on feminism, though I understand that blaming feminism for the various ills of modern life, including the supposed decline of manliness, is the point of your book.

Okay, I'm going to wind up and give you a chance to talk any minute now! Though I must also disagree with your idea that feminists are promiscuous and just want to have a lot of promiscuous sex, which is another of the big anxieties in the book. I'd say, rather, that what feminists, and women generally, want is *better* sex—quality, not quantity. Or first let's go for quality,

---

* In fact, this is an anxiety that's alive and well, and not just for neocons. See the February 2014 article titled "Does a More Equal Marriage Mean Less Sex" in the *New York Times Magazine* by the problematic LA psychotherapist Lori Gottlieb.

then quantity. But really, the more pressing issue is that we want female sexual pleasure to be taken as seriously as male sexual pleasure traditionally has been.

So, in short, what I'm saying is that the book's many anxieties—and it's *quite* an anxious book—are not really based in reality. They're psychosexual anxieties. They don't reflect the social situation we live in, which isn't to say they're entirely without basis. After all, anxiety's a real condition. But a good contrarian has to be accurate in describing the social picture, or his arguments just become silly rants.

So to conclude, feminism was never about forcing gender neutrality on the world, it was about ending gender hierarchies and the systematic forms of privilege that excluded women from important areas of social and public and professional life. But it's certainly understandable to me that the process of rebalancing the traditional distribution of power *would* be a source of male anxiety.

HARVEY MANSFIELD: This reminds me of my experience with Naomi Wolf [*apparently he meant that she wouldn't let him get a word in either*], but I'll begin by saying that I loved your book. In fact, your books, as I read your other one, *Against Love*, too. And I very much recommend that you [*to the audience*] buy them. Because this lady is a wonderful phrase turner, a beautiful writer and observer, and she's a thinker.

[*I was starting to feel bad about mocking his book; he really was a nice man.*]

I begin with that, and also I begin with the end of your book where you say that femininity and feminism are out of whack—I think that's definitely true. I very much agree with you there.

What you call the "female condition," I would call "female nature." The essential female condition, I think, is for women to be with men and to understand that men and women are different. So it becomes necessary to appreciate and to come to terms with those differences [*I'm starting to like him less*], whereas the female situation of today—meaning the effects that feminists have had on women—involve living in a society, which I call the gender-neutral society, where female nature is denied and gender differences are minimized as much as possible. By which I mean, your sex no longer gives you your rights, it doesn't give you your duties, and it certainly doesn't give you your place. That's a big difference from the past.

Now, it's true, there are lots of exceptions to this. But as an aspiration, society today wants sex to matter as little as possible [*most people would say "gender," but he prefers to collapse the two*], and therefore we want manliness not to exist. There isn't any respect or justification for the existence of a quality like manliness, which is specific to one sex only. Now, I don't say manliness is exclusively male [*indeed, he cites Margaret Thatcher admiringly as a paragon of manliness*], but it's predominantly male, something that men have.

How I define manliness is: "confidence in a situation of risk." Women have confidence, too, but they don't seek out risk the way men do. Or, better to say, the way some men do. Because manliness is a very *judgmental* quality. Some men have it, others don't, and those who have it look down on the men who don't have it. Whereas women, being excluded from manliness (even if that's not totally the case), are excused from being unmanly. So now we can go into some of the other differences between us.

KIPNIS: Well, one area about which you and I completely disagree is the really egregious claim that female modesty is a protection against rape. That's just silly. So is the idea that if women relied more on their femininity, men would be less violent because their protective instincts would be aroused. Also that if women played our roles more in accordance with nature, things would be better all around, because that would contain aggressive male behavior.

That's just a lack of reality, or a failure of social observation. It not only blames women for male irresponsibility—i.e., if we were more modest, then men wouldn't ever leave their wives and families in the lurch—it also blames us for the economic uncertainties inflicted on us all at this stage of capitalism. If women were more modest the family wage would be magically reinstated? Those evaporating pension plans would rematerialize? Look, the very idea that a woman can rely on a man for a lifetime of economic support is increasingly dubious, and that's just the new economic reality for all of us, no matter how demure and modest a woman is.

MANSFIELD: Well, let me say something about women's modesty.

KIPNIS: Please do.

MANSFIELD: I think women are naturally more modest than men. Men are more predatory or more adventurous in sex, and—it's true, a lot of women today try to match men here. And some of them succeed. Because a natural inclination is not something you *can't* oppose. So when I say women are naturally more modest, that doesn't mean that they can't be immodest, if they try hard enough. But they'll still always be fundamentally *more* modest, even when they don't want to be. Since this is the case, and since studies in social psychology tend to prove it, isn't it true that women, when they abandon the double standard in sexual morality—and that, by the way, is the only standard—are simply unhappier? Because once you abandon that, you abandon any standard at all.

KIPNIS: Well, mutual pleasure is one standard.

MANSFIELD: All right, okay—I agree with that. But it's not a moral standard.

KIPNIS: We probably disagree about that.

MANSFIELD: All right. But once you play the man's game, aren't you pretty likely to lose? You're going onto their ground when you try to compete with men in brashness. I think it's still the case that women like to be asked out, rather than asking out. For a man these days, sure it can be a great thrill to be asked out on a date by a woman. But, for the most part, women leave that to men, because when you ask somebody out you're taking the initiative, and I think men still want to take the initiative. They're the ones who make the first pass. You put your ego on the line. And I think a lot of women are more sensitive than men are. When a man gets slapped down he forgets it. It's not a great blow to his ego because there is probably something wrong with the woman who doesn't like him. [*Scattered laughter from audience.*] But it's different for women.

KIPNIS: You know, until pretty recently there were many more consequences for women when it came to sexual expression than for men. When Simone de Beauvoir, whom you discuss in your book, wrote *The Second Sex*, birth control was actually illegal in France—she had to go to New York to get a diaphragm. It's been less than fifty years that women have been freed from at least some of the consequences of sexual expression. So what women are "by nature," or whether women are more modest or equally immodest—I just think we don't yet know. Ditto the question of what women want from men, given that economic independence from men is also a fairly recent option.

MANSFIELD: As important as careers are for women, what's been more central in feminist thinking is this obsession with sex. And that's what's so wrong about feminism, and what has caused all the difficulties we see today and all the unhappiness that women have. Because most women do want to get married, and that's because they're smart enough to realize that a happy marriage is the most common and easiest way for a human being to be happy.

KIPNIS: I recall quoting a statistic in *Against Love* that only 37 percent of American couples who are married say they're actually happy. So your ideas about happiness in marriage may be overstated. But speaking of marriage, I was quite surprised to find such an ode to henpecking in your book, which comes up as part of your premise that women's role is to be a moral corrective for men. I may be wrong, but I'm under the impression that not many men are so on board with the henpecking plan.

MANSFIELD: Women and men are just happier married. What I actually said was that a happy marriage is the most common form of happiness.

KIPNIS: Ah, you're equivocating.

MANSFIELD: I didn't say *all* marriages are happy.

KIPNIS: And the percentages are diminishing by the minute.

MANSFIELD: Yes, I do think the number of unhappy marriages has been much increased by feminism. For example, the kinds of things we see on *Desperate Housewives*, where all the troubles of modern feminism are on view.

KIPNIS: [*Laughing*] Wait, are those women *feminists*? There's a certain slippage here between "women" and "feminists."

MANSFIELD: Right.

KIPNIS: When you say about *Desperate Housewives* that these are the emblems of modern feminism—where's the feminism? Sure they're women, they're suburban women living in suburban households. Maybe a few of them work outside the home, but again, what feminism?

MANSFIELD: I meant they show that feminism doesn't work.

KIPNIS: I see. Look, I know, you reject Freudian explanations, and let me preface what I'm about to say by reassuring you that I don't mean this in a personal way, but—

MANSFIELD: Uh-oh!

KIPNIS: —but there's just a real animus against women in your book, and it comes across in what you're saying here. You blame women for every problem of modern existence, including structural transformations that we're all struggling through. Let me cite a leading conservative, Francis Fukuyama, in *The Great Disruption*—just to show that I'm not somebody who thinks all conservatives are dumb—which is about the transformation to an information society, or postindustrial capitalism, or whatever you want to call it. His point is that this stage of economic development doesn't require gender differentiation for the new jobs that are available, especially technological or information-based jobs. Women's entry into the labor force and all the changes in the family starting in the '70s wasn't because of *feminism*, it was due to transformations in the economy, including the need for two incomes to maintain a middle-class lifestyle. He thinks feminism was an epiphenomenon of these economic transformations, not a cause of social shifts. In other words, don't blame feminists, blame capitalism! Yet all these economic forces somehow drop out of your argument and what you substitute instead is this nostalgic idea that aggression derives from body strength, and aggression underpins manliness, and manliness is the necessary quality for social creativity and energy, which accounts for who should run things—as if manliness is all that's necessary to put everything back on track.

MANSFIELD: Women, I think, just don't have the same kind of nonstop ambition that a man has. The "glass ceiling" is, for the most part, self-created by women. And I don't blame them for that because they realize that they're not going to be as happy as a man can be, sort of pushing ahead and never thinking about what's going on with the family back home. And that's why I think women are very wise in not trying to equal men for the same degree of income and career ambition. It's a good thing that people expect women to take care of their family more than they expect men to. And that's because women are better at it.

[*Moans from the audience.*]

KIPNIS: But creativity and intelligence are distributed equally between the sexes, so why are women supposed to relegate our creative efforts to the home, or to being moral correctives for men? Or let me try another approach. If you value women's moral contributions so much, then put your money where your mouth is. If things like child care and taking care of the home are such valued social enterprises, then reward people for doing them—give women Social Security or actual wages for these labors, which was one of second wave feminism's big ideas: wages for housework. Or how about wages for being moral correctives on men?

MANSFIELD: That's another one of my gripes with feminism—too much concern with money and calculation.

[*Groans and laughter from the audience.*]

KIPNIS: Okay, there's another issue I'd like to bring up, which is your idea about nature itself having some kind of moral force, that should in turn dictate our social roles. I have to argue with the idea that there are "natural" gender roles. To begin with, arguments proceeding from nature are completely suspect to me, because they're always completely selective. We like nature when it's a nice day at the beach; we don't like nature when it means being killed by a tsunami. We like flush toilets instead of having to defecate in the backyard, which would actually be far more "natural." We want to have happy sex lives without having to raise a dozen children. So even if there are physiological differences between the sexes that derive from nature, let's consider all these ways that technology and modernity have overridden "nature," in ways I believe all of us are in favor of.

MANSFIELD: In fact, the purists and the most radical feminists were very much hostile to motherhood and to anything which smacked of the physiological, or I might say the natural differences between the two sexes. The other thing feminists took no account of is manliness, or any quality specific to men that might cause resistance in them [to feminism], or that might require special allowances.

KIPNIS: That's a caricature of feminists. Or anyway you're picking and choosing which feminists you pay attention to.

MANSFIELD: I must admit, there are the later, more reasonable, less radical feminists. But their attention to manliness is about what they see as the defects of manliness, not the positive qualities, the assertive qualities, those qualities which have made men the leaders of all the great changes of the world.

[*Groans, laughter, and a smattering of applause from the audience.*]

. . .

MANSFIELD: Maybe some questions from the audience?

MAN IN AUDIENCE: I want to ask Professor Mansfield if it's true that manliness is a quality of men, if it has to do with risk-taking and aggression and strength, what will be the consequences to the conflicts among nations and entities when one is more feminine and one is more masculine?

MANSFIELD: Or what would be the consequences internationally for a country that was more feminine versus one that was more masculine? Well, we may be finding that out when we look at the decline or decadence of Europe—

KIPNIS: Because of all the women leaders, you mean?

MANSFIELD: Because of all the womanliness in their policies. Let me be less provocative and say that I perfectly well realize that men are responsible for most of the ills in the world and also for most of the remedies. So you look at the manliness of the Islamic hijackers, it takes a certain manliness—a corrupt or perverted manliness—to fly airplanes into buildings and kill people. Versus the manliness of the New York police and firefighters who went up the stairs of those buildings, knowing that they probably wouldn't come back down.

So yes, I think that manliness is responsible for the fact that the great preponderance of crime is committed by men. The great preponderance of the prison population are men. History's great tyrants are men. But men are also responsible for the kind of good which results from somebody standing up and taking a risk. So manliness is not simply aggression, it's also assertion—assertion of a point of justice, or a point of right. When that

point is a contest and when it takes courage, then it takes manliness to make that point.

KIPNIS: Your argument, once again, gets very slippery: whatever you disapprove of gets described as feminine, so the Euro-
pean welfare state is feminine because you're politically against
it. Whatever social institution you approve of, namely the culture of individualism, or a personal trait like courage, is manly.

MANSFIELD: But earlier you heard me praise the morality of
women.

KIPNIS: Yes, we're all very grateful!

MANSFIELD: Yes, I know you are, that's why I did it. There are
differences between men and women, and some of them are to the
advantage of men and some are to the advantage of women, and
sometimes it's good to have both. On the whole we need aggression but we also need caring. But it's just very unlikely that you're
going to routinely find one person who's both. When I say that
women are less aggressive than men, that's a generalization. A ste-
reotype. But most stereotypes, as I've said before, are true with
regard to sex.

KIPNIS: Like dumb blondes?

MANSFIELD: Dumb blondes are . . . a disappointment.

KIPNIS: There's a quote from Brecht, which I'll paraphrase
because I can't remember it exactly, it goes something like:
"It's impossible to understand the laws of gravity from the
point of view of a tennis ball." And in my view, we're all the
tennis balls at this moment. We're living through a period of
massive social and economic transformations, and both of our

books respond, in different ways, to this period of upheaval in gender roles.

MANSFIELD: You know, I'll defend you on this, because—

KIPNIS: My protector!

MANSFIELD: —you may not like it [*addressing the audience*]— but I think there's a lot of common sense in her books, and much less feminism than we've seen today in her manner. And she does recognize the obvious differences between the sexes and tries to come to terms with them, and she recognizes them in a very intelligent manner. I wouldn't give up on her.

I was left wanting to thrash him, but in a fond sort of way. After the debate, Mansfield shook hands with me and told me how wonderful I was. He couldn't have been more gracious. A short time later he invited me to Harvard for a conference he was holding on feminism (with a nice honorarium), but the prospect of having to play the role of its tireless defender and rehash basic principles exhausted me in advance, so I politely declined.

III

. . . . .

SEX FIENDS

Gropers

It's not that I don't take male professors seriously, far from it: these are a serious bunch of guys with vast storehouses of accumulated knowledge about often-arcane things, though it's no news that social graces aren't always high on the list. Ask a male academic what he's working on and too often he starts vying with Fidel for the longest monologue on record. He feels some compelling need to cram all the available space full of words, *his* words. Does he think you're interested? No, he's forgotten you're even there. Having posed this question on occasion when stumped for conversational topics at an academic reception or cocktail party—then been left shifting my weight from one foot to the other clutching a long-empty glass, praying for rescue or at least a refill—I've resolved to shelve such lines of inquiry. I feel especially bad for their students, forced to endure semester-long monologues delivered with all the charm of sawdust, though let me quickly add that some my best friends are male academics, and they're exempt from the above remarks.

But all in all, I like academic life. At its best, it's a big drawing room comedy peopled by awkward characters like me, bumbling around, causing offense in new and surprising ways. I also
love academic gossip, one of the great topics at academic con-
ferences, where, after delivering papers to dozing colleagues
from far-flung places, we gossip about other colleagues not in
attendance, especially the annoying ones. At one such recent
event, I was wedged between two acquaintances who'd formerly
taught at the same university. The wine was flowing; so was the
professional dirt. One had since moved on to more lucrative
pastures, and the other one was updating her on departmental
politics and personalities at the old place: whose book was fin-
ished, who had another job offer, whose tenure prospects were
looking grim. "What about Bob?" asked the departed one, delicately wrinkling her nose. "Just as bad," replied the other. "It's a
real problem." She explained to me, "We have this guy in the
department who . . . doesn't wash." They both laughed, almost
apologetically. "He *smells*." This was no mild odor apparently,
but a full-fledged stench. "It's worse if he gets excited about
something. If you get into an argument with him, watch out."
The departed colleague suggested that it was a form of aggression. He sounded like a skunk, able to release malodorous stink
bombs at will. "Time for an anonymous note," I proposed. "You
could make it sound like it came from a student—misspell
everything."

Bob comes to mind because stinky academic behavior has
been so much in the news lately, and the offenses of the male
professoriate continue to take such eye-rolling forms. The problem is that a slew of new behavioral regulations are being
imposed on all the rest of us in consequence. And it's all taken so
seriously now: some maladroit male professor gropes an under-
graduate, and instead of ridiculing the guy, or telling him to back

off, in today's climate it's practically mandated that the student become traumatized for life by the experience.*

The new terminology coined to address such occasions is making things even worse. Consider the "unwanted sexual advance": what tangled tales of backfired desires, bristling umbrage, and mutual misunderstanding lurk behind this sterile little phrase. In the right hands, such narratives once provided great raw material for comic or satirical treatment: look how obtuse humans can be in the throes of desire! What optimists we are about our charms and physical allures! But those deploying the new coinages find no human comedy in such situations. Forget bumbling pathos or social ineptitude—in these accounts, it's all trauma, all the time.

Let me offer an example of what I mean, since a detailed account of one such episode is contained in the charges leveled in a *New York* magazine cover story by feminist author Naomi Wolf against the literary lion Harold Bloom—a man of rather advanced years at the time of the article's publication—concerning a long-ago unwanted sexual advance. Despite the ancient vintage of the incident, the story created an international media stir. And by ancient, I mean it had taken place some twenty years before, when Wolf was in her senior year at Yale and Bloom was one of its celebrity professors. He had "sexually encroached" on her, she now charged, and she still wasn't over it.

The story goes like this: Wolf had asked Bloom to do an independent study devoted to critiquing her poetry, and he agreed to meet with her weekly. Unfortunately, these sessions failed to come off. Bloom, known for hanging out with his student coterie at a

---

* Just the other day I received a memo on new sexual misconduct policies at my university that referred to students who press harassment charges against faculty members as "survivors"—even prior to any finding on the accusation.

local pub, suggested getting together over a glass of amontillado to discuss the poems, but this never happened either. Bloom then invited himself over to dinner one night with Wolf and her two roommates—one of the roommates happened to be Bloom's editorial assistant. After dinner the roommates go off somewhere, Bloom and Wolf are sitting on the couch. Bloom clutches Wolf's sheaf of poems close and Wolf thinks she's finally going to receive a few pearls of insight from the illustrious scholar. Instead he leans over, breathing, "You have the aura of election upon you." Then he puts his hand on her thigh—a "heavy, boneless hand," as Wolf describes it, in a bit of literary-anatomical flourish. Wolf leaps up and vomits into the kitchen sink. Bloom leaps up and grabs his coat. Corking up the rest of his fancy sherry, he leaves, telling her on the way out, "You are a deeply troubled girl." They never met again; Bloom gave her a B for the independent study.

There's no doubt that being groped by someone you find unappealing can be disgusting and gross. And irksome—for maybe a day or two. Even a week. But when Wolf writes, decades after the knee-groping, that she's *still afraid* of Bloom, and that he'd played such a large role in her imagination that she'd stopped writing poetry after the encounter, you find yourself thinking that some crucial things are being left out of the story. What's being left out, I'd suggest, is first of all, the great man's pathos, and second, the complainant's own conflicted desires.

When Bloom had invited Wolf to come chat with him after she'd audited one of his famous courses, she was "sick with excitement" at the prospect, she wrote. He had an aura that was compelling and intimidating, he attracted brilliant acolytes, and Wolf wanted to be one of them. And let's face it: the sexual privilege that accrues to Important Men like Bloom accrues for exactly these sorts of reasons, which is why ascribing such scenes to male sexual rapaciousness alone doesn't explain enough. For one thing, it bypasses the inconvenient problem that power can be erotic, even when possessed by otherwise flawed and unappealing people, especially for those without power (and I'm speaking as a former fawning young student myself: this is not unfamiliar territory). What is to be done, short of a complete overhaul of the human psyche?

Maybe a more nuanced account of male power would be a place to start. Let's imagine, for instance, that some percentage of these otherwise flawed and unappealing Important Men were the guys everyone laughed at in high school or who've been otherwise dented on their journeys through life and now, having achieved some elevated standing in the world, find themselves on the receiving end of periodic adulation from those in positions of lesser power, for instance, their students. Even if these flawed men *should* bring the full measure of their maturity and moral judgment to bear, even if the erotics of power and sexual activity per se *should* be understood as two distinct things, it's not hard to see that rectifying those earlier injuries and humiliations might be the more pressing psychical priority.

What I'm trying to say is that, paradoxically, the trouble really starts when the idealized masculine icon fails to be phallic *enough*, when the icons turn out to be damaged and insecure themselves, when it turns out that Big Men also want validation from those they're supposed to validate. And for the acolyte, with so much hero worship driving the story, how could the Big Man *not* fail and disappoint in stomach-curdling ways? Oedipally speaking, a father figure in the erotic crosshairs is a complicated entity, so complicated that twenty years later the idealizer might still be rehashing the story. (Wolf has told this one in multiple venues by the way; see a previous rendition in her memoir *Promiscuities*.)

But even beyond the levels of mutual miscomprehension propelling these situations, what I've never understood about the phrase "unwanted sexual advance" is that it suggests the outcome of the advance should be known *prior* to that outcome occurring. Do we all announce our desires in neon letters on our foreheads? Do we even know beforehand what they actually are? Surely someone's occasionally caught by surprise, unexpectedly propelled from a non-desiring state into a desiring one by something in the moment, or the air, or the wine. I know it's happened to me, and I suspect I'm not alone. The point is, how can the advance-maker be expected to know ahead of time whether an advance is wanted or unwanted when desire itself isn't a stable condition to begin with? Just to be clear, I'm not talking about cases of ongoing unwanted sexual advances—or threats, or quid pro quo demands—otherwise known as "sexual harassment." I'm talking about regular human mating conduct, which often involves just . . . giving it a try.*

I realize that raising such questions puts me out of step with current thinking about how professors should relate to our students. Maybe I'm out of step because when I was in school hooking up with professors was just what you did; it was more or less part of the curriculum. Admittedly, I went to art school, and in a different era. Mine was the lucky generation that came of age in that too-brief interregnum, after the sexual revolution and before AIDS turned sex into a crime scene replete with perpetrators and victims, back when sex—even when not so great or someone got their feelings hurt—fell under the category of experience, not trauma. It wasn't *harmful*; it didn't automatically impede your education; sometimes it even facilitated it. This isn't to say that teacher–student relations are guaranteed to turn out well, but then what percentage of romances do?

---

* For the record, I strongly believe that quid pro quo harassers should be chemically castrated, stripped of their property, and hung up by their thumbs in the nearest public square.

To protect against such contingencies, colleges around the country have been formulating policies to regulate these situations and protect students against the sort of permanent injuries sustained by Wolf. ("Once you have been sexually encroached upon by a professor, your faith in your work corrodes," she writes.) My quarrel with these codes is that the vulnerability of students has hardly decreased under the new paradigm; if anything vulnerability is on the rise, because under the new "offensive environment" guidelines, students are encouraged to regard themselves as such exquisitely sensitive creatures that an errant classroom remark impedes their education, as such hothouse flowers that an unfunny joke creates a lasting trauma. And telling one may, by the way, land *you*, the unfunny prof, on the carpet or even on the national news.

Knowing my own propensity for unfunny jokes, I realized it was probably time to read my university's harassment guidelines, which I'd long avoided doing. When I finally buckled down and applied myself to studying them, I was interested to find that they were far less prohibitive than other places I'd been hearing about, at least when it comes to student–professor couplings: you can still hook up with students, you're just not supposed to harass them into it. How long before hiring committees at these few remaining enclaves of romantic license begin using this as a recruiting tool? *"Yes, the winters are bad, but the students are friendly."* However, we were warned in two separate places that inappropriate humor violates university policy. I've always thought inappropriateness was pretty much the definition of humor—I believe Freud would agree—but as thinking so probably meant I was clinging to gainful employment by my fingernails, I decided to put my name down for one of the voluntary harassment workshops they were running, hoping that my good citizenship would be noticed by the relevant university powers.

At the appointed hour, things kicked off with a "Sexual Harassment Pretest." This was administered by David, an earnest midfifties psychologist, and Beth, an earnest young woman with a master's in social work. The pretest consisted of a long list of true-false questions such as: "If I make sexual comments to someone and that person doesn't ask me to stop, then I guess that my behavior is probably welcome." Despite the painful dumbness of these questions and the fading of afternoon into evening, a roomful of people with advanced degrees seemed grimly determined to shut up and play along, probably aided by a collective wish to be sprung by cocktail hour. That is, until we were handed a printed list of "guidelines." Number one on the list was: "Do not make unwanted sexual advances."

Someone demanded querulously from the back, "But how do you *know* they're unwanted until you try?" (Okay, it was me.) Our leader, David, seemed oddly flummoxed by the question, and began frantically jangling the change in his pants pocket.

"Do you really want me to answer that?" he finally responded, trying to make a joke out of it. I did want him to answer, but also didn't want to be seen by my colleagues as a troublemaker. There was an awkward pause in the proceedings while he stared me down. Another person piped up helpfully, "What about smoldering glances?"

Everyone laughed, but David's coin-jangling was becoming more pronounced. A theater professor spoke up, guiltily admitting to having complimented a student on her hairstyle that very afternoon (one of the "Do Nots" involved not commenting on students' appearances) but wondering whether, as a gay male, *not* to have complimented her would have been grounds for offense. He mimicked the female student, tossing her mane around in a "Notice my hair!" manner, and people began shouting suggestions about other dumb pretest scenarios for him to perform, like sexual harassment charades. Rebellion was in the air. The man sitting next to me, an ethnographer who studied street gangs, whispered, "They've lost control of the room." David was jangling his change so frantically that it was hard to keep your eyes off his groin. I had to strain to hear what people were saying.

My attention glued to David's pocket, I recalled a long-forgotten pop psychology guide to body language that identified change-jangling as an unconscious masturbation substitute. If the very leader of our sexual harassment workshop was engaging in offensively public masturbatory-like behavior, seizing his private pleasure in the midst of the very institutional mechanism designed to clamp such delinquent urges, what hope for the rest of us?

Let's face it: other people's sexuality is often just weird and creepy. Sex is leaky and anxiety-ridden; intelligent people can be oblivious about it. Of course the gulf between desire and knowledge has long been a tragicomic staple: consider some notable treatments of the student–professor hookup theme—Coetzee's *Disgrace*; Francine Prose's *Blue Angel*; Jonathan Franzen's *The Corrections*—in which learning has an inverse relation to self-knowledge, professors are emblems of sexual stupidity, and such disasters ensue that it's hard not to read them as cautionary tales about the disastrous effects of intellect on practical intelligence. The implementers of the new campus codes seem awfully optimistic about rectifying the condition.

I wonder what the esteemed Professor Bloom, ferocious scourge of every "ism," would have made of our little gathering. I suspect he'd be against trying to corral the tumult of carnality into a set of numbered guidelines, and perhaps also more attuned to the powers of the weak. In fact, this was another question I'd wanted to ask David: Isn't it possible that the recipients of unwelcome advances wield *some* power in these situations—the power to reject and humiliate the advancer, at the very least?

Along these lines, Jane Gallop, a feminist English professor who's acknowledged seducing more than one of her professors while a graduate student, has said, looking back on her experiences, that sleeping with professors made her feel cocky. She wanted to see them naked, she says, to see them as like other men. Lots of smart, ambitious women were doing the same thing at the time, she points out (this would have been the early eighties)—it was a way to feel your own power, to *not* play out a victim scenario. No doubt in a better world where people didn't require such circuitous forms of validation, fewer such transactions would take place and everyone would have sex for only the right reasons (whatever these would be), but so far humankind has not evolved to this higher plane, or not to my knowledge.

It's not that I don't understand Wolf begrudging Bloom's clumsy attempts to employ her for the grubby purposes of masculine validation, but what she's ignoring about this scenario is that she had power over him too—because of her good looks and youth, to be sure, but they're hardly worthless currency in our culture. Perhaps especially so for those whom nature has chosen to deprive in this regard. The photos running alongside Wolf's article tell their own story: Wolf at twenty, rather gorgeous; Bloom, in an undated photo, one of the less attractive men on the planet.

As for the power Bloom wielded over Wolf, it wasn't because he was collecting a paycheck from Yale—there was no attempt to cash in there, no quid pro quo harassment. He took the "No" in stride and retreated to nurse his wounds. The power he had was his intellectual prowess, the power of his literary judgment: he was a charismatic learned guy, and Wolf wanted his approval (and wanted to be found attractive, she admits elsewhere). But when she writes about becoming sick with excitement when Bloom agreed to read her poems, it isn't really clear that either's fantasies were any more objectifying than the other. When Wolf insists that Bloom has power over her, what she doesn't get is that it's because she's in *thrall* to his power, not because he exercises it; in thrall to the phallic mythos she's also so deeply offended by. I fully agree that men have too much power, though what we glimpse here is the degree to which that power continues to be propped up by women's fantasies about masculine icons. What also gets left out of the story, at least in Wolf's telling, is that these fantasies are themselves a source of pleasure, even when not exactly borne out by reality.

What's equally excruciating about the whole imbroglio is that the power of youth and prettiness was so transfixing for the aging ugly man that he abandons all dignity and puts himself in such an untenably comic position. The levels of mutual misunderstanding approach condition of farce. At least having written an introduction to a new translation of *Don Quixote*, with its notorious projectile vomiting scene, Bloom, if anyone, would (one presumes) be able to appreciate the low comedy of his failed wooing of Wolf. And as for Wolf, having vomited on the Great Man's advances, can't she rest assured that she got her point across sufficiently twenty years ago?

Whether or not it's a brilliant move, plenty of professors I know, male and female, have hooked up with students for shorter and longer durations, though female professors do it less, and rarely with undergrads. (The gender asymmetries here would require a dozen further essays to explicate.) Some of these professors act well, some are assholes, and it would behoove the student population to learn the identifying marks of the latter breed early on, because post-collegiate life is full of them too. I propose a round of mandatory workshops on this useful topic for all students, though it seems unlikely that anyone other than me is about to sign this petition.

But here's another way to look at it: the *longue durée* view. Societies keep reformulating the kinds of cautionary stories they want to tell about intergenerational desire and the catastrophes that result, from Oedipus Rex to student–teacher dating policies.* The details vary; so do the kinds of catastrophes prophesized—once it was plagues and crop failure, these days it's psychological injuries. But even over the last half-century the story continues to be reconfigured. In the preceding era, it was the Freudian account that reigned for explanatory purposes: children universally desire their parents, such desires meet up with social prohibitions—the universality of the incest taboo—and become repressed. Neurosis ensues.

These days, intergenerational desire remains a dilemma, but what's shifted is the direction of the arrows. Now it's *parents*—or their surrogates, teachers—who do all the desiring: children are returned to innocence. (The recovered memory movement also has a lot to answer for here, having transformed a lot of perfectly adequate parents and nursery school teachers into molesters on the basis of therapist-induced accusations.) So long to childhood sexuality, the most irksome part of the Freudian story. So too with the new campus behavior codes, which also excise student desire from the story, extending the presumption of the innocent child well into his or her collegiate career. Except that students aren't children.

Recently, an erotically confused friend, a handsome sometimes-professor nearing sixty and separated from his wife, showed up for drinks with a twenty-five-year-old blonde in tow. She had

---

* In fact, my university's policies were further reformulated in early 2014, just as I was completing this book. Faculty and undergrads are now prohibited from dating or any other sort of consensual relationship, even when not in the same department.

long flowing locks and a Kewpie doll face. They'd met at a writing workshop he'd taught. "She's a little stupid," he confessed, sotto voce, when she went outside for a smoke. "But she has this . . . animal vitality that's really appealing."

He claimed to want to get back together with his wife. Well, maybe he did; he wasn't sure. "I like being married," he mused. "I do better when I'm married." I responded, possibly with a bit of an edge, that for someone who says he likes being married, he seemed to veer in the opposite direction. "I know," he said, abashed. He leaned closer and whispered, "I'm so fucked up."

I tried not to feel censorious, since who am I to feel censorious? "Is there a creative figure who has not had a desperately confused sex life?" asks Gilbert Sorrentino in *The Imaginative Qualities of Actual Things*. Part of me envied my friend's willingness to be so emotionally incoherent, and to find such willing accomplices at every turn. As for his student, an aspiring writer, I figured she was getting a lot of potential material out of it, not to mention a valuable educational experience.

Cheaters

If I'd been having an on-and-off-again affair with a married sports hero and discovered, to my dismay and chagrin, that a lot of other girls were simultaneously having affairs with the same married sports hero, would I feel justified in telling (and where possible, selling) my tale of romantic injury to the media? This is a question I found myself asking a lot when the marital woes of a certain world-class golf champion became a protracted national preoccupation, with embarrassing new revelations issuing daily from the media wing of his ad hoc harem. I suspect the answer in my case would be "maybe so"*—at least, I can understand how getting clobbered with photos of ten or twelve other mistresses and realizing you weren't as special and chosen as you'd thought, that you were actually one of a *small crowd*, might demand

---

* I was once on the verge of publishing an ex's letters along with a wittily acerbic running commentary until halted by a cautious editor, so I must acknowledge that there's no high ground for me to claim here. But as Robert Lowell famously included his ex Elizabeth Hardwick's letters in a book of poems, there were distinguished literary precedents for this kind of thing, or so I assured myself.

some score-settling. At least you'd want to straighten the media out on how you were different from all the rest of them. Classier, for instance.

But here's another question that crossed my mind. Did the married sports hero in question have some kind of unwitting *penchant* for sexual and romantic partners who would subsequently feel the need to share their experiences with the world? Is this now a type—not blondes or brunettes, but the garrulous? Or was the sports hero just a little willfully oblivious about certain facts of contemporary life, namely that it's a new ball game when it comes to celebrity sexual privilege nowadays? Maybe there's a tough message such guys need to hear (yes, this is largely a male club), which is that the fans and admirers most drawn to these high-wattage hookups appear to be the same cohort most inclined to sell you out later. Worse news still: this cohort may well include your current spouse. If I were a tabloid-worthy sports icon or any scandal-avoidant celeb, I'd want to note the correlation. Serial philanderers and sexual compulsives need to be better psychologists in the age of Twitter, as one suspects that psychological savvy rather than good luck alone is the quality that separates those who end up in national ignominy from those who don't.

In the interests of promoting a more emotionally attuned celebrity sector, I'd like to offer a few cautionary observations to all at-risk male celebs, at least those who haven't yet been caught in "compromising positions." To begin with, it's a tough world out there, my friends. Gone are the days when a Monica Lewinsky told *only* a dozen or so friends and relatives about her thing with the president. These days a dozen confidantes might as well be none for someone nailing a famous guy, which is something worth thinking about if you happen to *be* a famous guy, or hope to become one someday.

Also: these days everything is personal, but nothing is private.

Chalk it up to the rise of narcissism, the digital revolution, the tabloid media explosion, or all of the above, but the upshot is that how we perform our roles as selves in public has radically altered in a relatively short period of time, and one of the main symptoms is that what used to be the public–private divide has become so porous as to be almost indecipherable. We're increasingly conducting our emotional lives in public view. This has many sweeping social consequences, and one of them, sadly, is that the traditional entitlements of celebrity status come with new disincentives, namely that your one-night-standmate is likely to be tweeting about your performance or preferences before the sheets are even dry, or snapping naked cell phone photos of you while asleep, to deploy as necessary should you neglect to call the next day or otherwise disappoint (which you inevitably will).

To return to the case under consideration, what was it that the legendary Tiger Woods—who conducted himself in a not particularly elegant manner with a string of talky paramours (more than a dozen eventually came forward with their grievances, their reminiscences, and copies of Tiger's text messages where available)—might have missed about the women he was involved with? His wife too would soon come forward with her own grievances, reminiscences, and scrapbooks of painful marital memorabilia—we'll return to her shortly.

Let's put on our psychologist hats and ponder this question: what exactly *is* the allure of sex with celebs, especially married ones who'd prefer to keep your existence a secret (though maybe they'll text you next time they're back in town *if* they can get away)? No doubt there's simple animal attraction: celebs are frequently charismatic, they have an aura, sometimes they're even quite good-looking. No doubt there's the feeling of "a connection," a "special spark," though that often evaporates by morning. But the main benefit, as anyone with experience of such things knows, is that it confers *specialness* on the lucky recipient of the celeb's attention: "He/she could choose anyone, and he/she chose *me*."

In Keith Richards's memoir *Life*, a book crammed with sharp observations, I was struck by his passing remarks about the groupies who congregated at the hotel room doors whenever the Stones came to town. In contrast to some of his bandmates, Richards claims to have been indifferent to racking up sexual scores, though he makes use of these women nevertheless, occasionally for sex, but more often for other things. "They were providing a service . . . like the Red Cross. They'd wash your clothes, they'd bathe you and stuff." Most of them weren't particularly attractive, he notes. And though grateful for their ministrations, he still wonders why they were doing it.

It's a shrewd question: why indeed? Probably because people use sex for a variety of purposes, including as a curative, to assuage something, to feel a certain way about themselves. . . . This is fairly standard human behavior, and includes men and women both. Still, one doesn't wish to discount the excitement of hanging out with rock stars, but the entry price for these women was a certain amount of willing self-abnegation. Maybe more than a certain amount.

The problem with the groupie dynamic, at least from the savvy celeb's standpoint, is that someone who craves the proximity of celebrity limelight and feels confirmed by hit-or-miss attentions bestowed under less-than-egalitarian circumstances is also likely to be someone afflicted by greater-than-usual quantities of insecurity and self-doubt, yet hopeful that a bit of the limelight will magically rub off, improving life in some unspecified fashion. Unfortunately, it doesn't usually work that way, as the confirmation-seeker begins to realize the morning after, as the now mysteriously less-attentive celeb prepares to jet to the next city to greet the next admiring horde. Who wouldn't feel a teensy bit aggrieved and maybe even slightly vindictive when the requisite quotient of affirmation is withdrawn? In fact, it's probably those hoping to be lit up by contact with the limelight who are *most* likely to feel aggrieved and possibly vindictive in such conditions.*

Luckily for the aggrieved, between the new consumer recording technologies, the tabloidization of traditional media, and the international market for downfall stories, the world will be falling all over itself for the details of these complaints. The groupie dynamic has undergone a revolution from below. Slut-shaming is no longer directed at women alone, it's anyone's weapon to deploy, as we saw in Tiger's case, where public exposure became the tactic of choice for redressing power inequities. I'm not saying it was an entirely *successful* tactic, but it can inflict a lot of collateral damage along the way.

But back to our psychology tutorial. Who *are* these fans most likely to feel affirmed by bathing in a celebrity's aura, who experience it as such a turn-on or confidence builder that they're willing to abject themselves as necessary for a few hours of horizontal proximity? Studying the photo arrays of Tiger's past mistresses for clues about their inner lives does reveal certain commonalities. To begin with, there's an insistent sexiness—a lot of bikinis, tousled hair, pouting, and perilously low-cut outfits. Tiger favored a certain physical type, it was widely (and leeringly) noted: blondes, and the especially well-endowed, were heavily featured. But I'd like to suggest that it was actually a common *personality*

---

* "The stupid part was believing a 22-year-old can be strung along for 6 months, abandoned & trusted to keep quiet." This was a tweet by the college student who'd received the original crotch shots from then-representative Anthony Weiner that led to his resignation from Congress (see "Humiliation Artists"); she was speaking here about one of her successors, the young woman who revealed the texts that demolished Weiner's mayoral chances two years later.

type the photos displayed: women whose calling card is *hotness* and who aspire to get things back from the world on that basis—attention, affirmation, riches, and maybe even love, though willing to settle for whatever's on offer in the meantime.

I don't want to sound judgmental. Obviously we all work with what allures and talents we've been given in order to get things back from the world. But making hotness your chosen avenue is a more precarious route than others: it makes you a little interchangeable; newer models keep coming out. There's also a certain amount of misrepresentation involved: the advertised hotness isn't really about "liberated" sex at all, it's the far more traditional variety—sex as exchange value, to get something in return, i.e., the security of a man's steadfastness. When that proved unforthcoming in this case, two of the girlfriends were insulted enough to hire a lawyer to demand Tiger publicly apologize to them too, after he'd publicly apologized to his wife. These were mistresses with a vengeance—literally—and not about to be treated like anyone's backstreet girl. They'd been dishonored, and they wanted the wronged wife's prerogatives: a public grovel. (Some of them also wanted monetary damages.) Of course, there was another smidgen of limelight to seize too, and in this set, limelight is its own curative. But no doubt they did feel genuinely ill-used: injured by Tiger, they were out to return the injury.

It's not hard to understand anyone's disappointment in not being uniquely chosen, though what's missing from these grievances was any realistic understanding on their part of the man on the other side of the bed. Even through the opacity of the media carnival, you felt the poignancy of the situation, the poignancy of missed connections. What haunts these scenes is mutual misrecognition. The famously cynical quote from French psychoanalyst Jacques Lacan about love comes to mind: "Love is giving something one doesn't have to someone who doesn't want it."

It's a form of mistaken identity, in other words, inherently so: what we love are our projections. When transposed to the sphere of celebrity love, the same occlusions apply all the more—whether it's sexual encounters or product endorsements the celeb in question is being enlisted for. Tiger wasn't who the admiring throngs thought he was, and not who his corporate overseers needed him to be. Not the smooth, ruthlessly disciplined winner, not the pioneering role model, but as needy and conflicted as the rest of us. Everyone misrecognized Tiger, including, apparently, his wife, who arranged a cover story in *People* because she wanted the world to know she'd had no idea who she was really married to.

It was the first and last time she would tell her story in public, *People* assured its readers about the "fiercely private golden girl," Elin Nordegren. No one wants to minimize Elin's ordeal, but it's one of the paradoxes of our age that someone can be referred to in all apparent earnestness as "fiercely private," even while in the midst of retailing her private pain in a mass-circulation periodical.

Now, if *I* were a philandering sports celeb's soon-to-be ex-wife, even if I were really steaming (as I'd have every right to be), wouldn't I prefer to distinguish myself from the motley, mewling pack of "other women" and conduct my revenge in private? Isn't that what hundred-million-dollar property settlements are for?

Not anymore. Wronged spouses having their day in the press, "taking back their stories" in the aftermath of their husbands' sex scandals: it's the melodrama of our time. Melodrama is a genre that hasn't fared so well of late otherwise—the histrionic sufferings of a Joan Crawford or Bette Davis look campy now, having been expropriated by drag queens and recycled as bitter irony. But wrap the suffering in a layer of real-life scandal and you're back in business, which is where the betrayed wives of politicians and celebrities come in, armed with their brave stories and hindsight-tainted wedding photos. Note the familiar cast of characters: the quivering damsels in distress and the dastardly men who toy with them—it's the melodramatic imagination updated. No doubt there's something reassuring about the timelessness of these roles: she's the perpetually wronged victim, he's the devil incarnate or today's secular equivalent—a sex addict, a serial adulterer, an incurable narcissist. As in the current story, with the messy complexities of modern marriage retold as a shipshape morality tale of innocence and guilt.

According to the *People* profile, Elin was practically a candidate for immediate canonization: a "golden girl," a near-saint. The salvation-versus-damnation theme prevailed throughout the story. "I've been through hell" were Elin's words. "But I survived." Melodrama's signature is its overwroughtness—everything that can't be spoken of directly finds a backdoor way of sneaking into the story, in the guise of stylistic excess. Think of Douglas Sirk—the crashing music and swooping camera movements of *Magnificent Obsession* or *Written on the Wind* signaling the return of the repressed—and compare to the moral Manichaeism of Elin's *People* appearance.

The article kicked off with a full-page photo of the exceptionally blond former model (she hails from Stockholm) posed in a darkened room, chin on hand like Rodin's *The Thinker*, staring thoughtfully into the distance. A shaft of light shines through parted curtains, illuminating her hair and features, symbolizing hope—the new life of dates and degrees (she's back in college) that await her. Or maybe it's the newfound self-illuminations that her husband's betrayals have forced on her? Whatever that shaft of light symbolized, you couldn't help noticing how insistently the artfully styled visuals, along with the text itself, kept returning to the darkness-versus-light motif, another of melodrama's big preoccupations. "She is putting her darkest days behind her," confirmed the article's subhead, in case anyone missed the point. That the dark days suffered by the exceeding fair Elin were instigated by a dark-skinned man—in the multi-racial Tiger's designation, "a Cablinasian"—whom she's also putting behind her, added an awkward racial subtext to the marital melodrama. Did no one notice this?

Or maybe obliviousness was the prevailing condition on everyone's part in this story, every step of the way. Why *would* anyone think a talent for hitting a small ball into a hole with a long stick correlates with honesty or self-knowledge? Unfortunately, deficiencies in such traits made Tiger an inadequate corporate shill as well as a bad husband—there went $22 million in product endorsements overnight. He was definitely a big disappointment when it comes to the country's fantasies about the monogamous inclinations of sports legends, though wouldn't you have to be pretty credulous to bank on such fantasies in the first place?

And what of the saintly Elin: what of her fantasies, her credulity? Stepping into the public spotlight for the first and last time in *People*, the former model and former celebrity wife wanted the country to know that she'd been blindsided by her husband's affairs and never suspected anything. She knew the man she was married to very little, it seems. Though to be fair, Tiger turned out to be a more multi-layered personality than his fans, his corporate sponsors, or even his wife had any incentive to recognize. But then what use would a conflicted sports icon be to any of them?

As anyone who's been married (or simply been in the vicinity of a married couple) will attest, marriages are emotionally awkward arrangements between two people who frequently turn out to have wildly different needs and desires. Here's a hypothetical marital situation: one person likes sex and the other doesn't. Or once did, but doesn't much feel like it currently. Hardly an uncommon plight, according to anecdotal evidence. Isn't this a form of betrayal too? I'm not saying it was the case in the marriage under discussion, since I have no idea. I'm just saying that in the actual world we inhabit, not the one where the forces of darkness battle the forces of good, sometimes it's harder to know who's a saint and who's a sinner than melodrama would lead us to suppose.

Coupledom is a pact two people make to attempt to know one another and create a life together, but it's just as important to overlook things too. A certain amount of strategic myopia is required, or the marital enterprise would be in even worse shape than it is. Getting the balance right is tricky. Knowing someone too well can kill desire: boredom and irritation result. Knowing someone too little can lead to nasty surprises. It's one of the conundrums of modern coupledom, or call it a "challenge" if you prefer. How *do* you know who this person you're married to is "underneath"? And if you do learn everything there is to know, penetrate every secret crevice, how can you possibly continue?

It's a cliché to say that you never really know what goes on inside someone else's marriage, but the hard truth is that you never entirely know what's going on in your own: the most familiar spouse can betray you horribly, even when there's no other person in the wings. The forms of spousal betrayal I'm thinking of include the quotidian ones, which no one entirely eludes—getting fat, getting boring, getting old, and then dying, the biggest betrayal of all. Stepping out on someone is only the most dramatic instance of all the ways there are to be a disappointment to a mate, though it's the one around which every anxiety seems to cluster. But while we're at it, why not hurl a few condemnations at the less melodramatic betrayals too?

Look, I'm not saying I particularly want to be cheated on, though it's probably happened. If I sound cavalier about it, I suppose it's that I have a certain soft spot for restlessness and unruly desires, for wanting more as an ontological condition. Or for not knowing *what* the hell you want. I can understand the impulse to experiment with other emotional and sexual possibilities than domestic coupledom always delivers, though big messes certainly can ensue. But we live in complicated times and no one here's a saint. Probably no one much wants to live with one either.

Self-Deceivers

The philosophical literature on self-deception is not incredibly helpful if you're trying to learn how to avoid the condition. A recent examination of the topic begins with the following example: "A survey of university professors found that 94% thought they were better at their jobs than their average colleague." Are university professors exceptionally adept at self-deception or is it an endemic condition, the author (a professor himself) wonders. Yes and yes, but what does that tell us? Maybe that the extent of your own self-deception is one of those dog-chasing-its-tail questions no one's capable of answering—how would you know that the answer you came up with wasn't just another instance of your talent for self-deception?

I came to be perusing this useless genre of pseudo-expertise because I was writing a book about scandal and why people keep blowing up their lives in such flamboyant ways on the national stage, acting out their weird psychodramas and tangled antisocial desires, generally leading to grisly forms of humiliation. Society gets vengeful when its norms are violated—a fact you'd think would require a rather skillful form of forgetting to ignore, since it's one of those basic truths of social existence. Still, despite the many disincentives there's no shortage of humans lining up to do it all the time, fueled, it seems, by this fateful capacity for self-deception.

As we know, many of those in line are male politicians who, despite their buttoned-up demeanors, keep getting exposed to the world in farcical sexual situations. Or it's our habit to treat these episodes as farce: the late-night comedians go to town, the pundits take a jesting tone. Even so, there's nothing so uproarious about being the butt of late-night comedy; it's more like the modern equivalent of a town square pillory. It's not being shunned the exposed politician has to fear, it's being turned into a hapless schlemiel and getting *laughed* out of town.

Take the former presidential candidate and one-time vice presidential nominee who turned out to have been stepping out on his much-revered cancer-stricken wife, even fathering a love child with the other woman before finally terminating his presidential campaign. This was John Edwards, who'd billed himself as the model family man, then betrayed his family in the arms of a New Age twit everyone agreed was far inferior to his wife, then lied when asked about it, then hedged, then split hairs about the timing of the affair, then said that his wife's cancer was in remission at the time (as if that mattered), and to cap it off accused himself of narcissism and egotism during his televised mea culpa. As an apology, this backfired.

Because it's difficult to make embarrassing things go away on the Internet, it's actually still possible to find a number of so-called webisodes from the Edwards campaign online, shot and produced by the woman Edwards finally admitted to having the affair with. You can even hear her on the sound track asking coy questions of Edwards and giggling at his answers. Though there's some ambi-

guity about when the affair started, what's not in dispute is that
the affair-mate had no prior video production experience when
Edwards put her on the campaign payroll. Pretty clearly they
were sexually involved while she was shooting these videos of
him; clearly he knew that what was being recorded would be
posted on the Web for the world to see, and also knew—*at some
level*—that if these facts became public, it would decimate his
shot at being leader of the free world, which for a while didn't
look entirely impossible.* So the stakes were, arguably, high.

For the student of self-deception, these webisodes are quite a
trove of research material, especially the one on the subject
of . . . "authenticity." We track Edwards to various political ral-
lies, we're with him relaxing on his campaign plane in a back-
stage, unbuttoned view of the man behind the glossy posters. So
what should we make of it when Edwards says, to the camera:

> I've come to the personal conclusion that I actually want the
> country to see who I am, who I really am. I don't know what
> the result of that will be. But for me personally, I'd rather be
> successful or unsuccessful based on who I really am, not based
> on some plastic Ken doll that you put up in front of audiences.
> That's not me, you know?

Even for those of us who don't care to sermonize about other
people's sex lives, or who admired Edwards's position on the
wealth gap, it's hard not to be mortified by such a flamboyant

---

* In fact, many of Edwards's positions now look politically prescient. *Atlantic*
columnist Peter Beinart used the occasion of progressive New York mayor Bill de
Blasio's 2014 inaugural address to recall that it was Edwards's "Two Americas"
campaign theme that renewed Democratic interest in economic inequality after
Clintonism pushed the party rightward. Beinart faults Democrats for airbrushing
Edwards from party history while borrowing his anti-poverty proposals to ride
the post–Occupy Wall Street momentum.

performance of self-contradiction on such a national scale. Political cynics will say that whenever a politician talks about authenticity he's sure to be lying, but here Edwards is also erecting the scaffolding for his own beheading, which is unsettling no matter how cynical you are. No doubt this accounts for the jokes. Levity at least forestalls having to look too closely at any similar propensities of one's own.

But there's another reason philosophers are interested in the question of self-deception. When we joke about the latest bimbo eruption, we're not just trading views on sexual morality, we're also having an implicit debate about how consciousness is structured. Where you come down on Edwards reveals what philosophers would call your philosophy of mind.

For instance: one of the more widespread explanations of Edwards's behavior was "hubris." This was shorthand for the view that Edwards was lying, knew he was lying, knew that exposure of his lies would mean downfall, thought he could get away with it, and simply miscalculated. Those who hew to this story are taking the position that all mental activity is conscious, and all facets of the mind are transparent to itself. Self-deception per se doesn't exist for this camp; those who engage in what might *look* like self-deception are actually fully conscious of what they're doing—they're *deliberately* acting badly and they know it; they're just hoping not to get caught.

Opposing the hubris camp we have what might be called the "compartmentalization" camp. Compartmentalization proponents would say that Edwards wasn't *consciously* deceiving his audience. He both knew what he was doing, and didn't: the main person he was deceiving was himself. This camp would lean toward a more Freudian account of the psyche: there are forms of knowledge that are accessible to one part of the psyche and not to another. Two incompatible beliefs can coexist because humans are eternally and irrevocably split, making complete self-mastery an impossibility. To a compartmentalization theorist, a hubris-camp joke like "He couldn't keep it zipped" is itself an instance of compartmentalization, a symptom of the same forms of split consciousness it means to condemn. Fooling yourself about the supremacy of self-knowledge makes you a walking example of compartmentalization.

At this point our picture of how the mind is structured becomes necessarily more ornate, because if you're lying to yourself, who's the self doing the lying, and who's the self being lied to? And if we're so essentially split-uppable, such bifurcated beings, is this any way to live—not knowing at any moment whether one part of you is actively working to sabotage the other?

Watching Edwards proclaim, in that "authenticity" webisode, that he wants the country to know who *he really is,* I don't doubt that he meant every word of it. He wanted the country to see who he was, while at the same time knowing that he was a man with a career-destroying secret—after all, the secret was sitting across the aisle from him on the campaign plane, holding the camera that was recording those very words. Yet if two such opposing forms of knowledge can coexist autonomously in the same psyche, then none of us is in such great shape from a self-preservation standpoint. It's not that Edwards is a stupid guy. What he failed to grasp was his own capacity for self-deception. But let's face facts: aren't any of us capable of massive forms of self-betrayal every waking hour of the day?

Here's someone who would disagree. One of our most adamant anti-compartmentalizers was the philosopher Jean-Paul Sartre, whose explanation for what afflicted Edwards (were he still around) would probably have been "bad faith," a condition to which he devotes a well-known chapter in his otherwise unreadable tome *Being and Nothingness*. Sartre vigorously rejected the whole premise of the Freudian unconscious: not only is it possible to consciously believe something in the face of evidence to the contrary, but in his terms, lying to yourself is *always* a conscious decision. The Edwards authenticity webisode would be doubly ironic for Sartre, since for him bad faith is the quintessential form of inauthenticity—you're appropriating a false notion of self, because you're knowingly participating in your own self-deception. You're refusing the radical possibilities of freedom he thinks are obtainable, and instead acquiescing to life in a social cage.

He offers up a series of charming little vignettes to illustrate the point. The most famous one involves a waiter in a café whose movements are just a little too precise, who "comes toward the patrons with a step a little too quick. He bends forward a little too eagerly; his voice, his eyes express an interest a little too solicitous for the order of the customer." What's he up to? "He's playing at being a waiter in a café," Sartre diagnoses. Why? Because this is what his customers want, so the waiter becomes alienated from himself, and imprisoned in his social role.

What's so charming is how closely observed and present this waiter seems—it's like you're there witnessing the scene yourself, as Sartre, a major café-goer, obviously was on many occasions. In addition to the waiter immortalized in his semi-comic impersonation of waiter, there's another much-cited example: the story of a young woman who consents to go out with "a particular man" for the first time and pretends not to notice his sexual advances. As Sartre explains, she actually knows quite well what the man's intentions are, but puts off deciding what to do about them, "concerning herself only with what's respectful and discreet in his attitude," instead of admitting to herself what's really going on.

Sartre charges the young woman with bad faith. Why? Because she wants to see these compliments and attentions as about her *personality*, even though she knows it's not her personality that interests the guy. But for her to recognize "the desire cruel and naked would humiliate and horrify her." Yet there's no reward for her in just being respected either, Sartre guesses. So she refuses to recognize the guy's lust for what it is, because in the end she doesn't actually know what she wants. Next comes a lengthy analysis of what ensues when the man pushes the situation further by holding the woman's hand, which calls for a decision: if she leaves her hand there she's saying yes to his advances, but if she pulls it away she breaks the charm of the moment. So she tries to postpone a decision as long as possible. "We know what happens next," Sartre mocks. She leaves her hand in his, but she pretends not to *notice* what's happening to her hand and starts expounding about Life instead, in lofty, sentimental ways. Meanwhile her hand stays inert, "between the warm hands of her companion—neither consenting nor resisting—a thing."

"We shall say that this woman is in bad faith," reproaches Sartre.

But who *is* this "particular man"? Is *he* in good faith? This question we somehow never get around to. Given Sartre's reputation as one of the twentieth century's great chasers of women, known to discourse freely on his career as a seducer in the same suavely knowing tones of these vignettes, perhaps we can be forgiven for engaging in a bit of biographical fallacy. Critic Louis Menand writes of Sartre's legacy in these matters: "As one would expect of the great advocate of transparency, he discussed his reasons [for pursuing women] frankly"; these reasons, he frequently said, were primarily the pursuit of female beauty. (He saw it as a way of developing his aesthetic sensibility.) As Menand quotes Sartre: "First of all, there is the physical element. There are of course ugly women, but I prefer those who are pretty. . . . Then there is the fact that they're oppressed, so they seldom bore you with shop talk. . . . I enjoy being with a woman because I'm bored out of my mind when I have to converse in the realm of ideas."

Well, that *is* frank. So let's be equally frank. One recalls on reading this that Sartre himself was not exactly physically prepossessing, in fact he was rather ugly—about five feet tall, wall-eyed, and with a serious indifference to hygiene, Menand notes, though he could still rely on charm and charisma as seduction tools, not to mention his status as a famous philosopher. Who needs hygiene when you have charm and charisma? Still, the ugliness had to rankle for someone so attuned to aesthetics. Indeed, in his wonderful memoir about his childhood, *The Words*, Sartre writes devastatingly about the shattering effect that realizing that he was ugly had on him. Always having been an adored child, at age seven his grandfather snuck him off to get his long blond ringlets cut off. This turned out be a grave error since without the hair as distraction, his ugliness became undeniable. From that point on, the mirror showed him what a monster he was—and from that point on he became a little imposter, he writes, overplaying his part "like an aging actress" to court his family's attention and adoration.

The description of childhood bad faith, of impersonating an adorable child, is one of the more brutally honest descriptions of childhood I've read—reading it brings horrible memories rushing back of performing for adults as a child myself, in hopes of a few crumbs of love. (In my case I pretended to know how to read by memorizing a Peter Rabbit picture book at the age of three or so, including exactly where to turn the pages, astounding any relative who was willing to sit through a rendition.) You feel, reading *The Words*, that this is an author who knows about inauthenticity firsthand, and is well equipped to diagnose it in himself and his fellow sufferers. Of course, here you'd be wrong.

Back to that uncooperative young woman. According to Hazel Rowley's superbly gossipy excavation of the self-mythologizing relationship between Sartre and Simone de Beauvoir, Sartre spent two years trying and failing to seduce a seventeen-year-old student of Beauvoir's named Olga (Beauvoir had already slept with her); he finally gave up and spent another two years trying to seduce her sister Wanda, at which he eventually succeeded. These campaigns do sound awfully similar to the seduction vignette from "Bad Faith." If the seducer's position in the story is less thoroughly investigated than that of the young woman, if it's taken for granted that her acquiescence is his due, the reader finds herself pondering whether there's something simply inaccessible to "philosophical" knowledge here. That is, whether contrary to Sartre's theories, *not* everything in the mind *is* completely available to consciousness.

When Sartre pronounces, of the recalcitrant young woman, that she possesses "a certain art of forming contradictory concepts which unite in themselves both an idea and the negation of that idea," I have a hard time seeing why it's *she alone* who's in bad faith. The whole thing reeks of falseness. To put it bluntly, he's deceiving himself.

To a philosophical philistine like me, what we have are a lot of words being thrown at the world's most banal situation, which is a disparity in levels of sexual attraction between two people, something the less-desired person both knows and refuses to know. When Sartre proclaims that this woman is free, then rebukes her for refusing the possibilities of her own freedom—while simultaneously attempting to pinion her within the most constricting forms of submissive femininity—you feel the narrator is desperate to persuade you that if she *were* fully conscious of her freedom she'd jump on her companion and start humping away.

How is it that Sartre, who doesn't believe in self-deception, doesn't allow himself to see how self-deceptive he's being?

I'm pressing a bit hard on this example because it's astounding how enshrined it remains to this day in the literature on self-deception, with succeeding generations of philosophers circling around it still like some sort of talisman. Take an anthologized article by a philosopher named Bruce Wilshire that opens by retelling Sartre's vignette: "A young woman is invited out by a man who she knows will try skillfully to seduce her. This troubles her. Nevertheless she accepts his invitation, for she finds him attractive. . . ." But nowhere does even Sartre say that the woman finds the man attractive. What a strangely reverent alteration, as if to retroactively airbrush the great man's grotesqueness! Wilshire does update the vignette with a little psychologizing of his own: "She colludes with him to relieve herself of responsibility," because "in all likelihood she's acting out archaic responses to early authority figures who molded her mimetic life."

Well, maybe so—after all, she's a fictional character and I guess anyone can say what they like about her mimetic life. And since this isn't 1970 and I'm not Kate Millett, I'll refrain from grumpy commentaries on the gender assumptions and asymmetries that stud our philosophical inheritance since it would sound too obvious at this late date. But I suppose this example especially rankles because I myself am old enough to recall once being called "bourgeois" for not wanting to go to bed with an unattractive man (who also seemed to think sexual compliance was his due), which felt not unlike being accused of bad faith. I too was playing a false social role, he was saying, just like the comedic waiter in the café.

The setting was some kind of Marxist summer institute we

were both attending, though even then the accusation sounded musty; it smacked of party meetings and sectarian correctness. Doris Lessing's early Communist stories are full of scenes like this—male radicals recriminating their female counterparts for their bourgeois failings, and indeed, my miffed accuser was a left-wing South African academic, so perhaps a bit behind on North American advances in female autonomy. He'd been caught up in real political struggles back home, his tales of which impressed me. But being called bourgeois stung—nowadays I'd readily agree and whip out my Barneys charge card, but back then I always felt I had something to prove. Still, the label didn't make me change my mind. I just wasn't attracted to him, though it wasn't something I was capable of saying.

Or that's how I remembered the evening. Not long ago I happened on two rather passive-aggressive letters from the man in question, in a stash of old correspondence. In the first, which arrived out of the blue some six months after the institute concluded, he lamented that something had been left unconcluded between us. "Perhaps writing is closer to ping pong" he wrote elliptically, and I recalled that we'd spent part of an evening playing ping-pong (being Marxists, we were housed in some kind of shitty dormitory). I suppose he meant to imply something about playfulness in lieu of heavy scenes, though the letter wasn't really playful, it was somewhat cutting, even though written in an elegiac mode. He mused about why he hadn't called me before he'd left the States; wondered why he was bothering to write now, and concluded with hopes that my work was going well but who knows, "time slides by so rapidly these days, maybe you're into something else—perhaps even babies." It didn't take an expert in textual analysis to read the condescension, though there was also a pleasing postscript about his sharp images of me not having been blunted by time.

Or I suspect it would have pleased me—I wanted to be found attractive, and being memorable would suffice—though apparently I sent a caustic reply, reminding him that he'd called me "bourgeois" and chiding him for being such a leftist cliché. I don't actually have a copy of my reply, but he quotes portions of it back to me in his second letter, which was addressed "Dear Unsuspecting Young Thing," and chides me for chiding him for what he calls "mere linguistic excesses." "Tsk tsk" he faux-reprimands himself, then accuses me of trying to transpose our encounter into the battle between "Feminism" and the "Male Left," where according to him, we hardly belonged. "I mean, what we have here is Laura and J——, after an evening of food, drink, ping pong, and artful sparring, unaccountably in Laura's room, sitting on Laura's bed, when WHAM! By the effect of some camera obscura, we are transposed onto the larger screen of History itself. Don't our protagonists feel a mite swallowed-up by the clash of battle so skillfully sketched?"

What kind of Marxist thinks we aren't actors on the screen of history? However, it was another line that caught my attention. "What *was* Laura doing on the bed that evening after all?" This was followed by a few semi-pornographic speculations about the memories that might have been ours to treasure, in lieu of the paltry ones we were stuck with, if only I hadn't been so unwilling to lose my cool.

On my bed? What *was* I doing sitting on my bed with this smug and annoying man, I now wonder. The locale seems awfully equivocal, given that I was so definitely not attracted to him. And did he take my hand, like Sartre's seducee? Did I pretend not to notice? As to how we found ourselves on this bed, I've conveniently forgotten the relevant details. The problem is that for a long time this story had been one of my comedic staples about the blunderings of the male Left: the time an unattractive Marxist accused me of being bourgeois for not wanting to go to bed with him. Clearly I needed a new anecdote for my repertoire.

But back to Sartre. If the most canonical example of bad faith seems so steeped in bad faith itself, reeking of sexual disappointment with an overlay of self-exoneration and preening, can any of us ever know our own motives sufficiently to avoid falling into similar swamps of failed self-knowledge, particularly when it comes to sexual pride or your own good opinion of your charms and acuities?

"People who believe that they are strong-willed and the masters of their destiny can only continue to believe this by becoming specialists in self-deception," says David, the unreliable narrator-seducer of James Baldwin's *Giovanni's Room*. This would be a great insight, but it's one no authentic self-deceiver ever actually manages to voice—it's Baldwin's insight into his character, not the character's into himself. But what other options are there for any of us, such predictably unreliable narrators of our own lives? One solution: we become experts on the existence of these traits in others. On which point, I suppose my rebuke of Sartre isn't so unlike his rebuke of the unseducible young woman. He reproaches her, I reproach him, my South African confrère and I reproach each other. . . . And we all heartily condemn John Edwards, who made us watch those horrible televised tributes to his authenticity.

What strikes me most in the Edwards webisode is how *happy* he looks, beatific even. He was adored by the woman holding the camera—certainly more than he was at home, by all accounts—and it shows. Clearly it was mutual, and mutuality is hard to come by. Knowing that one true thing, he forgot everything else.

Other people's failures of self-comprehension make such tempting targets: you get to forget all similar occlusions of your own, while luxuriating in the warm bath of imaginary self-awareness.

IV

. . . . .

HATERS

The Critic

When I was growing up there was a game called Spanking Machine. I believe it may have originated as a birthday party ritual, and from there took on a life of its own. The rules were simple. One person was designated the spankee, the rest of us played the role of spankers. Everyone lined up in a row, back to front, legs apart to form a tunnel. The spankee started at the front of the line, then scurried through the tunnel on hands and knees while getting spanked on the butt by each spanker in succession. The spankee then took up his or her place at the end of the line, whereupon the first spanker became the spankee and scurried through the tunnel on hands and knees while getting spanked on the butt. And so on, until everyone had a turn.

That was the whole game. There were no scores, there were no winners or losers, there was just a lot of spanking. At that age we were all switch-hitters, so to speak—no one had yet formed fixed preferences or roles. The only variation was that occasionally someone spanked too hard, and someone else ran home crying.

What I find myself wanting to know, from the vantage point of "adult" life, is whether these mysteriously gratifying childhood reveries are simply abandoned in the course of growing up, or do such impulses live on? Maybe my Chicago neighborhood was a particular enclave of polymorphous perversity, but you don't have to be Freud to notice just how many opportunities for spanking and being spanked persist into later years. No, I don't just mean in the privacy of your boudoir or the pages of publications with names like *Mommy Severest*, but deflected elsewhere, into—let's say—"higher-minded" realms. Cultural pursuits, for instance.

In other words, could those have been professional critics-in-training, the over-zealous spankers? I ask because somehow it's these childhood games that spring to mind when I reflect, these many decades later, on the lofty enterprise we call Criticism.

It's not exactly news that a lot of symbolic violence gets played out in the form of cultural judgments, but there's one figure in particular whose work really slams the point home. This would be the literary critic Dale Peck, who propelled himself to the epicenter of book world buzz for his savage reviews of fellow writers; those he finds overrated or not up to his standards are publicly eviscerated, their entrails hung from a pole in the public square (in other words, the back pages of the *New Republic*). Nor has he feared to mete out slashing appraisals of literary luminaries like David Foster Wallace, Philip Roth, and Julian Barnes, admirably intrepid when it comes to attacking superior writers in inferior prose.

But it was one rather shrill sentence in particular—"Rick Moody is the worst writer of his generation"—that set the book world to fretting about the ethics of criticism, since it seemed more like butchery than run-of-the-mill critical vehemence. You got a slightly queasy feeling about the whole thing, the impression that more was going on here than should be. Such questions resurfaced when some of the most scathing reviews from Peck's oeuvre were collected in a winkingly titled volume, *Hatchet Jobs: Cutting Through Contemporary Literature.*

Needless to say, the initial problem *Hatchet Jobs* raises for critics is the temptation to unleash on Peck the same brand of slashing aggression he himself practices, which wouldn't be that difficult since whatever aesthetic program he might be promoting amidst all the invective is actually pretty mysterious. True, the madly hyperbolic style can feel invigorating next to more measured reviewers, but if the so-called literary criticisms being exacted seem capricious, and personal agendas seem to overtake aesthetic judgment, it does raise certain larger questions about the critical enterprise itself: namely, what sort of subterranean impulses are generally being gratified here?

It's not that critics don't do a lot of routine breast-beating about what criticism is for, and how much it should hurt. Whether critics are *too* mean is a perennial topic. Or alternatively, too soft-hearted—"Are novelists too wary of criticizing other novelists?" was a question the *Times' Sunday Book Review* asked two reviewers to hash out in its pages in mid-2013. This was right around the time that another self-described hatchet-job critic, Lee Siegel, announced that he was giving up negative book reviews, despite the fact that takedowns got the most attention. He'd lost his taste for it; and besides, there were real-life consequences for people. He named Dale Peck as one in the slaughterhouse-style lineage he'd chosen to abandon.

For Siegel it was a question of ethics, but what I'm more interested in here is the psychology of the critical enterprise. Given how compulsively self-revealing Peck himself has been in print— frequent confessional interviews, a family memoir, constant self-reference in the reviews themselves—I propose that we read *Hatchet Jobs* not for its literary assessments but as a case study on the psychogenesis of critical aggression.

Let me begin by extending my appreciation to Peck for vol-
unteering himself for the project, even if this wasn't precisely his
intention. But the fact is that Peck published two books within a
year of each other: *Hatchet Jobs* and a quasi memoir called *What
We Lost*, about his abusive father—and the father's abusive parents, and the culture of sadism that reigned in the family—and
any halfway attentive reader can't help noticing that the two
books are mirror images of one another, begging to be read in
tandem for what each explains about the other.

The family story is a pretty miserable one. Peck grew up poor
on rural Long Island, the son of an alcoholic plumber who beat
up a succession of wives and killed the family dogs with a
wrench when there wasn't enough money to feed them. His
mother died when he was three; she was seven months pregnant
at the time. Peck speculates that violence was involved. When his
father discovered his son was gay, he beat him up too, though
the physical violence was usually directed toward his wives, with
the son as onlooker. Apparently the father had spent his own
childhood being sadistically abused, especially by his mother,
who had quite a talent for it: her creative sadism included making him unscrew the hose from the washing machine so she could
beat him with it and forcing him to eat plates of uncooked beef
fat. She told him she wished he were dead rather than a sibling
who had died. Writing *What We Lost* was Peck's attempt to come
to terms with this multigenerational legacy of violence.

Some of this biographical backstory I've distilled from interviews, and some from *What We Lost*, though it can be a bit oblique.
"Based on a true story" according to its cover, it's largely a story
about child abuse, and the child being abused is Dale Peck. But
not Dale Peck the author—the main victim is Dale Peck's father,
also named Dale Peck, though at first we don't actually know it's

anyone's father, since for the first part of the book the beaten child is referred to ambiguously, only as "the boy." If this is confusing, prepare for more confusion, because there's another Dale Peck—an earlier son that Peck Sr. had with his former wife. This Dale Peck was ferried away by his mother; later Dale Peck, the author, came along and was assigned the same name. All these Dale Pecks get beaten—some are beaten by a mother, some by a father, some by other children, but in all cases, viciously. The plot goes something like this: A boy is beaten, he escapes being beaten by going to live with an uncle, then returns to the family home only to be beaten once again. You might say that a certain preoccupation with *beating* governs the narrative—everywhere you look it's a hall of mirrors reflecting these various Dale Pecks, either getting beaten or doing the beating themselves.

At this point, anyone who happens to have read Freud's 1919 essay "A Child Is Being Beaten" will have alarm bells clanging in her ears. Freud reports that watching other children get spanked turns out to be a frequent childhood erotic fantasy for both boys and girls, or so a number of patients told him (in fact, one such fantasizer was apparently his daughter Anna, whom Freud analyzed when she was in her early twenties, there being a dearth of other psychoanalysts around at the time). This fantasy, shameful yet immensely pleasurable, is often a favorite masturbation accompaniment, sometimes to the point of obsession. The most intriguing part of the essay, at least from a bibliophile's point of view, comes in an aside—often the case with Freud—when he notes that *books* frequently stimulate beating fantasies, particularly certain scenes in the sort of well-meaning books often foisted on children for the purposes of their moral education. In his day, *Uncle Tom's Cabin* was a particular favorite in this genre.

As the fantasy gets unraveled in analysis, all sorts of

permutations emerge: first it's the father beating another child—a hated child like a brother or sister; then it's the father beating the child who's doing the fantasizing, but in a way that's highly pleasurable; in another version, it's some other authority figure like a teacher doing the punishment. All of which provides, as Freud puts it delicately, "a means for onanistic gratification." Yet by this point even Freud's confused—what to make of this shadowy half-remembered world of childhood fantasy, where love, spanking, gratification, sadism, and masochism merge, roles are interchangeable, spectators become victims, pain is pleasure, and being beaten means being loved? He finally comes to think the origin of the whole thing is buried sibling rivalry, and the fantasy ultimately about that most thwarted of quests: a parent's unalloyed love.

What's remarkable is how closely Freud's world of beaten children chimes with the world of beaten Dale Pecks in *What We Lost*, with its unwieldy confusion of names and roles, sadism and masochism, pain and pleasure, adults and children—it's almost as though Freud had read Peck's book.

At least Peck's version of the story comes with a redemptive coda. Dale Peck Sr. eventually stopped drinking and reformed. The son who'd once suffered abuse and humiliation at his father's hand reconciles with him in Part 2, and the two set off on a road trip to the uncle's farm where Dale Peck Sr. had once passed a brief respite from violence. In Peck's world, like Freud's, violence is ultimately a route to love, and *What We Lost* is supposedly the outcome: the son's attempt to come to terms with a legacy of paternal abuse. Of course, at another level it's also a chance to pummel Dad, since what else is a writer doing in a beating scene but administering one to a character? All the better that here it's the author's formerly terrorizing father, returned to the vulnerability of childhood by the now all-powerful son, and finally getting what he should have gotten long ago.

. . .

What We Lost may be an attempt to come to terms with (or avenge) paternal abuse, but now we come to the world of thrashed and chastised writer-siblings critic Peck surrounded himself with in later life, as he administers those notorious "hatchet jobs" in the companion volume. Reading Peck's criticism alongside the quasi memoir, you're left thinking that maybe he hasn't so much abandoned abuse scenarios as turned book reviewing into an opportunity to enact new ones.

Let's return to that notorious opening sentence from Peck's review of Rick Moody's memoir *Black Veil*. After pronouncing Moody the worst writer of his generation, he continues, "Like all of Moody's books, it is pretentious, muddled, derivative, bathetic." Reading on:

> Moody starts his books like a boxer talking trash before the bout, as if trying to make his opponent forget that the only thing that really matters is how hard and how well you throw your fists after the bell rings. . . .
>
> For me, the beginning of a Rick Moody book is a bit like having a stranger walk up and smack me in the face, and then stand there waiting to see if I am man enough to separate him from his balls.

It's as though there's not enough manhood to go around. A private logic begins to emerge: Peck reads Moody's book as a threat to his masculinity, so he has to hit back, and hard enough to settle the question. Others may cozy up to a book with cup of tea in hand, but reading for Peck means two men pinning each other in sweaty headlocks and trying to beat each other senseless.

Of course, given *Black Veil*'s subject, you see why this

particular book might exacerbate manhood dilemmas for Peck. To begin with, it's framed as an investigation of Moody's patrilineal line and moneyed background (not surprisingly, class resentment figures heavily in Peck's review, which includes mocking Moody for a lengthy given name that Moody doesn't even use). But *Black Veil* is also a meditation on the innate violence of masculinity and heterosexual privilege. What was the subject of Peck's then-forthcoming book, *What We Lost*? A meditation on manhood and violence, and the story of three generations of male Pecks. Even the subtitles echo one another. Moody's is "A Memoir with Digressions"—or as Peck sneers in his review, "a so-called 'memoir with digressions'"; Peck's was billed "Based on a true story." These are two writers mining the same stream.

Moody's book must have struck close to home for Peck, and home for him means irrational violence. Which may explain why his inflamed criticisms of Moody are not exactly the height of coherence, as when he mocks Moody's critique of traditional masculinity as a form of political correctness—a surprising position from someone whose father beat him up for being gay. And mocks Moody's confessions of vulnerability, including his obsession with being raped, as if vulnerability were inherently shameful—as it was *chez* Peck—finally winding himself up to the knockout punch: Moody's book "is so awful that it is easy to see the book as in league with the very crimes [racism, sexism, homophobia] that it seeks to redress." Why not the Holocaust too?

Given the timing of the book and the review—Peck said he spent several months reading through Moody's work prior to reviewing it—it's likely he was writing about Moody and his father around the same time: thwacking one, redeeming the other, replaying the brutal parent as he was revisiting the brutality of his own and his father's childhoods. The blurred boundaries between the two are all too evident. When Peck writes, ostensibly of

Moody, "His much touted compassion strikes me as false (in his fiction he makes his characters suffer in order to solicit your pity) . . ." or "[Moody] hides his despondency behind literary bravura and posturing," who are we actually talking about? There's also something alarming about a critic so eager to slap down another writer for the crime of shrill prose, while so oblivious to the shrillness in his own. Has no one ever mentioned to Peck that the shriller the accusation, the more it reeks of projection?

Sibling rivalry isn't exactly an unfamiliar critical mode, especially when writers are reviewing writers whose work overlaps with their own, though here it's as if the sibling under review had been magically propelled back in time to the brutal childhood world of *What We Lost* and subjected to its ritual abuses, alongside all those unlucky Dale Pecks.

Clearly the question of his own manhood preoccupies Peck, expressed—as is often the case—as a horror of femininity. Other critics are "a bunch of pussies," a characterization he'd apparently do anything to avoid being branded with himself. Yet in his many interviews, he veers between aggression and woundedness, self-aggrandizement and abjection. He's been misunderstood, all he cares about is literature—but other writers get bigger advances! Enacting his critical jihads is "the only way I can get people to realize how good my books are . . . and honest to god, I don't think that's hubris." As he explains in the afterword to *Hatchet Jobs*, he's the real victim—wounded by these books he's been asked to review, deceived by all the fame grubbers. Though he's also deeply worried about bad reviews himself. He's prone to overblown statements like: "The books I've published are among the best books published in the last 10 years." *What We Lost* is "impossible to review badly." He designates himself "one of the

best writers around." He doesn't like being at the center of attention, he says—midway through yet another interview.

As to who's the better writer, Moody or Peck, or more of a
man, on the all-important question of who can separate whom
from his balls, all we can hope is that there are plenty of Band-
Aids on hand should they try—really big ones. But I don't want
to limit this inquiry to Peck alone: his talent for re-creating abuse
scenarios in his prose just makes the critical dynamic so wonderfully unsubtle. The real question is whether this is a generalizable
condition, whether in Peck's story we find the hidden template
for the "hard-punching" critic generally. What's most notewor-
thy in Peck's confrontation with Moody isn't the content of his
rapier judgments, it's the portrait of the critic that emerges, with
literary criticism a stage on which to enact interior dramas. Pun-
ishing imagined inferiors, subjecting victims to the same capricious abuses you yourself have suffered—well, here's a creative
solution to a stored-up history of persecution, at least: counter-
acting its effects by deflecting them elsewhere.

The point is that punch-outs preoccupied Peck a long time
before Moody happened along; Moody was just collateral damage. Meting out blows while suppressing empathy for the victims
at least offers the advantage of not having to experience your own
history of vulnerability. Or that's how it's said to work with battered children who beat their own offspring. The knowledge that
they themselves were once beaten *is* conscious—it's the suffering
it exacted that you hide from yourself. And from the ranks of
the brutalized, writes psychologist Alice Miller, are recruited the
most reliable executioners, prison guards, and torturers, who are
compelled to repeat their own history because they've so totally
identified with the aggressive side of their psyche.

It's something of a cliché these days that brutalized children
risk growing up to brutalize their own children, but what's less

discussed are the countless ways there are—and venues in which—
to administer brutality. What makes it tempting is the temporary
distance it offers from your injuries and vulnerabilities; the com-
forting fantasy of imperviousness from pain.

There's always something perversely gripping about people
acting out these kinds of psychodramas in public. If the residues
of Peck's family horror show seep into his brand of critical vehemence, it's one of the things that makes his writing compelling, I
suppose. It's his habit of transforming these propensities into
moral high-grounding that wears thin—for instance, his sancti-
mony about Philip Roth's attitudes toward women in *American
Pastoral*. ("It's not really the misogyny in this passage that takes
the breath away as much as it is the gynophobia. . . .") Then you
come across Peck interviewed at *Gawker,* referring to a previous
interviewer as "Elizabeth Manus or man-slut or whatever her
name was," and to Jessa Crispin, who runs the amusing website
Bookslut, as "ditch-dirty stupid," and renaming her "Jessa Crisp-
Tits." Does writing critical takedowns exempt the critic from his
own standards, or is Peck playing another game: doling out cas-
tigation and then soliciting it, re-creating the circle of abuse that
gives *What We Lost* its narrative structure and makes reading
Hatchet Jobs mostly feel like more of the same?

Of course Peck is hardly the first writer to enlist culture as a
means of repairing life's injuries and redeeming its losses: transforming unlivable emotions into other idioms and forms is a large
part of what gives culture its emotional resonance. (As Pico Iyer
puts it about the writer's task: "He has to plunge so deeply into
his recesses that he touches off tremors that find an echo in a
reader.") If Peck captures the prosecutorial tone of the emotionally abusive parent, obviously this would resonate for far too
many of us: the language of criticism *is* first learned in families,
our earliest reviewers, after all. Who escapes unscathed from

these lovely scenes? Brutality is forever tempting for just such reasons, offering the opportunity to disavow your own history of vulnerability and injury while reproducing it in others.

Following *Hatchet Jobs,* Peck announced that he'd be giving up the pain game; he planned to stop writing criticism. Like his father, he intended to reform. But can his readers? If big-stick literary criticism fills a certain cultural niche, if there's a certain nasty pleasure in watching other kids get beaten up in "hard-hitting" reviews, no doubt it's because these proclivities aren't Peck's patrimony alone.

Even though I've never thought of myself as a particularly hard spanker, I suppose I sent a couple of kids home crying in my earlier reviewing days, and in my own book-writing career, I once got punched so brutally that it left me reeling and gasping for air. (Another version of pretending invulnerability is the proclivity for especially vicious reviews by younger women of other women writers.) In the real world, where a lot of critics also write books, one day you're dishing it out and another moment you're taking it. It can be just as psychically complex for any of us as for Peck: are you avenging your own book's last bad review in the book review you've just been assigned to write? Cleansing yourself in the crystalline waters of your high-minded literary judgments, where nothing can really ever quite meet your standards? And there's always rampant careerism to factor in.

It sometimes happens that you encounter a victim of one of your critical spankings in social settings. It happened to Peck when he ran into the jazz critic and novelist Stanley Crouch, whose last book Peck had reviewed a bit unfavorably (*"Don't the Moon Look Lonesome* is a terrible novel, badly conceived, badly executed, and put forward in bad faith; reviewing it is like shooting fish in a barrel"), at a restaurant in the Village. Crouch approached his table, asked, "Are you Dale Peck?," introduced himself, shook Peck's hand, and while still clasping it with one hand, slapped him twice in the face with his other one. (This was reported online by various sources, including Crouch's lunch companion, the writer Z. Z. Packer.)

You'd think that Peck would be getting used to this kind of thing, but maybe not. One night I was out to dinner with a friend at another restaurant in the Village where you're apt to run into writers. Which is what happened: my friend recognized a friend of his as we were being shown to our table. We stopped, they hugged, the friend's friend in turn introduced us to her dining companion, who stood up from the table. The dining companion was Dale Peck. My friend introduced me. I had, by that point, published an earlier version of the remarks above in *Slate*, and when I stuck out my hand automatically, Peck refused to shake it. I stood there for a moment, hand awkwardly outstretched, then lowered it, breaking into a slight sweat.

I suppose I can understand him being unwilling to shake my hand, though having doled out far more than a lifetime's share of critical abuse in his day, I did think he was being a bit thin-skinned.

Men Who Hate Hillary

Here's what happened the last time Hillary Clinton ran for president: she drove men wild. Well, *certain* men. Especially certain men on the Right. You could recognize them by the flecks of foam in the corners of their mouths when the subject of her candidacy arose. And they're already girding themselves for the next time around, because there's something about Hillary that just gets them all worked up.*

But what exactly? Despise her they do, yet they're also strangely *drawn* to her, in some inexplicably intimate way. She occupies their attention. They spend a lot of time thinking about her—enumerating her character flaws, dissecting her motives, analyzing her physical shortcomings with a penetrating, clinical eye: those thick ankles and dumpy hips, the ever-changing hairdos. You'd think they were talking about their first wives.

---

* At the moment she has yet to announce for 2016, though it's assumed she will. The head of the Republican National Committee has already promised to go after the "rough stuff" and run ad campaigns that will be "very aggressive."

There's the same over-invested quality, an edge of spite, some ancient wound not yet repaired. And how they love conjecturing upon her sexuality! Or lack of, *heh heh*. Is she frigid, is she gay? *Heh heh*. Yes, they have many theories about her, complete with detailed forensic analyses of her marriage, probably more detailed than their thoughts about their own.

My point is that you can tell a lot about a man by what he thinks about Hillary, maybe even everything. She's not just another presidential candidate, she's a sophisticated diagnostic instrument for calibrating male anxiety, which is apparently running high these days. Understandably, given that the whole male–female, who-runs-the-world question is pretty much up for grabs. Face it: the possibility of a woman in the White House creates a certain frisson; how could it not? The historic distribution of power between the sexes is being revamped, power is a subject that cuts deep, and the male psyche is feeling a little embattled. Change hurts; loss rankles. Thus defenses are mounted, which—as any human with the usual repertoire of human emotions probably knows—can take some pretty convoluted forms.

Let me pause to confess that I haven't been the world's hugest Hillary fan myself—I'm not crazy about her politics, and her campaign stump speeches put me to sleep last time around, though she's grown on me since her Secretary of State stint. (Her defense of international abortion rights *is* rousing.) The problem is that I *don't* find her fascinating, which makes me even more fascinated by the passion of the guys who get so twisted up in knots about her. Of course, the Hillary haters assure us they don't hate Hillary because she's a powerful woman—they're not Neanderthals!— they hate her because she's *Hillary*. By attacking her they're just refusing to kowtow to political correctness.

Despite the reassurances, you suspect there's more to it than that. Hillary's ascendancy—to the Democratic ticket or ultimately the presidency—will be proportional to how much she vexes men. Despite all the platitudes about gender progress and "how far women have come," a certain obdurate level of anxiety persists between the sexes. The problem is that it's less permissible to discuss such anxieties, precisely because of all the progress. We're far too enlightened to be debating whether a woman *should* be president—that would be antiquated and discriminatory. So the qualms must find more creative routes of expression.

As our tour guides into these subterranean psychical thickets, I've enlisted a selection of Hillary's right-wing biographers to lead the way, or more specifically, a selection of authors obsessed enough to write entire books about a woman they detest, while still being lucid enough to find a commercial publisher. Unfortunately this excluded self-published works like *Hillary Clinton Nude: Naked Ambition, Hillary Clinton and America's Demise* by Sheldon Filger, but even the painfully repetitious title screamed for the interventions of a professional editor, and life is short. I also declined to read any books that came with voodoo dolls; sadly this ruled out *The Hillary Clinton Voodoo Kit: Stick It to Her, Before She Sticks It to You!* by Turk Regan, but as fuming tirades were in no short supply, I felt that I could afford to be choosy.

Biographies, even bad ones, are the record of a relationship, and sometimes that relationship just goes sour. A few self-reflective biographers have admitted as much: Thoreau's biographer Richard Lebeaux has commented that writing the book was like a marriage, and not always the smoothest of marriages, "not without some stormy arguments, separations, and passionate reconciliations." For whatever reasons, Hillary's biographers are especially prone to the marital mode. She seems to attract a certain type: guys with a lot of psychological baggage, emotional intensity, and messy inner lives. As we'll see, there are a lot of stormy arguments in these pages too, though fewer passionate reconciliations. Mostly it's a litany of injury and accusation, the sort of thing you tend to hear in couples with unhealthy levels of attachment.

What I'm saying is that reading these Hillary bios, you feel you're learning as much about the authors as you do about her, possibly more. So let's turn that spotlight around, shall we? After all, what's sauce for the goose. . . .

The obvious place to begin is with R. Emmett Tyrrell Jr., author of *Madame Hillary: The Dark Road to the White House*, since if Hillary's biographer-foes sound like embittered ex-husbands, in Tyrrell, founder and editor-in-chief of the far-right *American Spectator*, we're fortunate to have a biographer who's occasionally mused in print about his *actual* ex-wife. So who gets it worse—Hillary or the ex? Actually it's a toss-up. Indeed, Madame Tyrrell and Madame Hillary share an uncanny number of similar traits. Hillary's a self-righteous, self-regarding narcissist, "a case study in what psychiatrists call 'the controlling personality,'" and assumes the world will share her conviction that she's always blameless. Compare with Tyrrell on the soon-to-be ex, from his political memoir *The Conservative Crack-Up*: "She resorted to tennis, then religion, and then psychotherapy. Finally she tried divorce—all common American coping mechanisms for navigating middle age." When Tyrrell worries that suburban women will secretly identify with Hillary's independence and break from their husbands' politics in the privacy of the voting booth, clearly suburban women's late-breaking independence is territory he has cause to know and fear.*

Hillary's disposition is dark, sour, and conspiratorial; she has

---

* Feminists have long been Tyrrell's favorite punching bag in the *Spectator*: "disagreeable misanthropes, horrible to behold, uncouth and unlovely . . . burdened by a splitting headache, halitosis, body odor, and other ailments too terrible and obscure to mention." It's a bad thing about me, but I confess this made me laugh.

a paranoid mind, a combative style, is thin-skinned, and "prone to angry outbursts." Whereas the ex–Mrs. T., we learn, was afflicted with "random wrath"; and as divorce negotiations were in their final stages, threatened to make the proceedings as public and lurid as possible. Hillary has "a prehensile nature," which makes it sound like she hangs from branches by her feet. (Tyrrell has always fancied himself a latter-day Mencken, flashing his big vocabulary around like a thick roll of banknotes.) And while he nowhere actually *says* that his ex-wife hung from branches by her feet, the reference to protracted divorce negotiations probably indicates that "grasping"—the definition of prehensile (I had to look it up)—is a characterization he wouldn't argue with. When Tyrrell writes of Bill and Hillary that there was an emotional side to the arrangement, with each fulfilling the other's idiosyncratic needs, as we see, he's been there himself.

Threatening ex-wives, property settlements, bad breath—not exactly lighthearted stuff. Tyrrell at least tries to be amusing about it, in the sense that love transformed into hatred can be amusing, in a bilious, horribly painful sort of way. Not so with Edward Klein, author of the bestselling *The Truth About Hillary,* and a tragically humorless type. When Klein rants, "As always with Hillary, it was all about her," note the rancid flavor of marital over-familiarity—he's really just *had it* with her. He's practically venomous. Though he's also so suspicious of her sexual proclivities that unintentional humor abounds: he's like an angry Inspector Clouseau with gaydar. The inconvenient fact that there's no particular evidence Hillary bends that way dissuades him not. Thus we learn that Hillary went to a college with a long tradition of lesbianism (Wellesley), where she read a lot of lesbian literature, and two of her college friends would later become out-of-the-closet lesbians, and later, some of her Wellesley classmates were invited for "sleepovers" to the White

House. (Get it? *Sleepovers.*) In 1972, a Methodist church magazine she subscribed to published a special issue on radical lesbian
and feminist themes edited by two—you guessed it—lesbians. In
college, her role models were feminists who refused to wear pretty
clothes, and sometimes appeared mannish; her White House
chief of staff was also mannish-looking. Though according to
Klein, Hillary never much liked sex to begin with. Sounding like
a Monty Python rendition of a Freudian analyst, Klein speculates about a fight Hillary once had with a college boyfriend
about not wanting to go skiing; skiing, says Klein, "might have
been a substitute for an honest discussion about her sexual frigid-
ity." The episode ended with Hillary retreating into "icy silence."
Get it? *Icy.* (He also quotes Richard Nixon, of all people, who
said that Hillary is "ice cold.") Yet Klein reports that Hillary had
a torrid affair with Vince Foster, the deputy White House coun-
sel (and her former law partner) who later committed suicide.
This would make her a frigid closeted bisexual adulteress, for
anyone keeping track.

In his preface to the paperback edition of *The Truth About
Hillary*, Klein does attempt to weasel out of some of his more
incendiary allegations, claiming mysteriously that the "exaggerated rumors" about the hardcover edition—that it claimed Hillary's a lesbian and Bill raped his wife—"were blatantly untrue."
Huh? Because this is indeed the book that has Bill Clinton, on a
Bermuda vacation in 1979, telling some guys in the hotel bar that
he was going back to his room to "rape my wife," and this was
how daughter Chelsea was conceived. Perhaps Klein means that
he just quoted a lot of imaginary gossip rather than asserting such
allegations himself. True, it's his rhetorical strategy throughout
the book to employ others as mouthpieces for his sleazier innuendos, as when he imagines the West Wing staff gathered around
the water cooler asking one another:

Was it true they slept in separate beds?

Were there any telltale signs on the presidential sheets that they ever had sex with each other?

For that matter, did the Big Girl have any interest in sex with a man?

Or, as was widely rumored, was she a lesbian?

The italics are Klein's. If it's a handy truism that constant sexual innuendos mask a discomfort with sex, then Klein is one uptight dude.

But there's just so much sexual baggage among these guys generally, not to mention rather mixed feelings about the female body itself. When Klein writes of Hillary's lower regions that though she's "a small-boned woman from the waist up, she was squat and lumpy from the waist down, with wide hips, calves, and ankles," the blatant bodily aversion in the phrase "squat and lumpy" isn't just a disagreement with her health care plan. Klein's concentration on Clinton's physical appearance is so microscopic that you fully expect to turn the page and find an index of her moles, accompanied by a close reading of what they indicate about her moral insufficiencies.

None of this is exactly a testimonial to his deep self-acuity. Or very attractive propensities in a man, it must be said. Though maybe he's unconsciously identifying when he writes that Hillary had "always thought of herself as an ugly duckling," and particularly hated her body, which caused her to neglect her personal appearance as a young woman, and go around dressed like a hippie in shapeless clothes, and with hair that looked like it hadn't been washed for a month. Or secretly commiserating about her feeling "so hopelessly unattractive that she did not bother to shave her legs and underarms, and deliberately dressed badly so she would not have to compete with more attractive women in a contest she could not possibly win." I feel compelled to note, if we're going down this path, that—having seen a few photos of the author—this is a man who can't have felt entirely secure about his competitive mettle on this score either.

Hillary's physicality really does loom large for her biographers. Tyrrell too spends many passages mocking her youthful hairdos, down to the thick eyebrows, which once "would have collected coal dust in a Welsh mining village." In other words, she's an overly *hairy* woman, in addition to everything else. Hairdo, eyebrows—thankfully we're not privy to data on the condition of her bikini line. Tyrrell sounds like an aspirant for the Vidal Sassoon endowed chair on the Clinton-hating Right when he concludes that Hillary's "search for the perfect hairstyle has finally been resolved into a neatly elegant businesswoman's coiffure" and that she "seems to have turned her hair into a major strength." He also concedes that Hillary "flirts well" and has evolved into "a handsome woman." Klein gets in a few digs on this point himself, as you'd expect, benevolently mentioning that Hillary's the kind of homely woman whose looks have improved with age, then trotting out an anonymous medical expert to testify that she's been "Botoxed to the hilt."

You get the feeling that outsized female personalities both repel and attract Klein: note that his previous biographical subject was Jacqueline Onassis, another woman with a charismatic straying husband, by the way. Klein is one of those guys who snidely notes the cubic poundage of any oversized woman in the vicinity: Monica Lewinsky (who "had gained a lot of weight" and "was bursting the seams of her thin, sleeveless summer dress"), Bill Clinton's deputy chief of staff Evelyn Lieberman ("overweight"), and his Arkansas chief of staff Betsey Wright ("heavyset"), not to mention Hillary herself, whom Klein refers to

throughout his book by the nickname "the Big Girl." But hold
on—it turns out there's a gynecological explanation for those
lumpy legs and ankles, since Klein quotes yet another "anonymous medical authority," who speculates that Hillary may have
contracted an obstetric infection after giving birth to Chelsea
that resulted in chronic lymphedema, a condition that causes
"gross swelling in the legs and feet." Forgetting that this diagnosis is utterly speculative (and as far as I can tell, nowhere else
confirmed), Klein goes on to inform us that lymphedema con-
tributed to Hillary's pre-existing self-image issues, observing that
she tried to cover up the alleged lumpiness with wide-legged
pants. (Was she supposed to wear leggings on the campaign
trail?) You have to give Klein credit: it's not every biographer
who approaches his subject with calipers and a speculum. It's a
clammy job, but I guess someone had to do it.

No, Hillary doesn't elicit the best in her foes. On the sexual
creepiness meter, Klein gets some stiff competition from Carl
Limbacher, who writes for the far-right news outlet NewsMax
and is the author of *Hillary's Scheme: Inside the Next Clinton's
Ruthless Agenda to Take the White House*. Here's another biographer a little too keen to nose out the truth about Hillary's sexuality. In fact, Limbacher comes up with an even darker picture
than Klein's if that's possible: Bill Clinton is a predator, Hillary
digs it, and this is the key that unlocks her character. If Hillary
didn't literally hold down the victims while Bill did the deed, she
was complicit nonetheless—"a victimizer who actually enabled
her husband's predations," since "a woman with half the intellect of Hillary Clinton would understand that she's married to a
ravenous sexual predator at best—a brutal serial rapist at worst."
At least he compliments her intellect. I'm dying to know what
Limbacher imagines Hillary's wearing when he fantasizes about

her in the henchwoman-to-rape role—her *Ilsa, She Wolf of the SS* outfit or the navy-blue pantsuit.

But Hillary really only stuck with Bill because he was her springboard to power—or wait, maybe it was because "her state of denial was so extreme as to suggest some sort of psychological impairment." Then he says that Hillary had to suppress evidence of Bill's sex life, especially any suspicion that he liked rough sex, as some of his accusers implied, because this might "raise questions about her own private peccadilloes." It's not entirely clear what "peccadilloes" Limbacher is referring to, though elsewhere he says insinuatingly that Vince Foster was Hillary's "intimate friend." He forgets to offer any evidence.

As we see, the problem for Hillary's biographers isn't that a woman's aspiring to be president—none of them mount an actual argument against women as presidential candidates. The problem is that Hillary's a *deformed* woman. She's a sadist, a victim, asexual, a dyke—maybe all at once. Taking the measure of Hillary's perverted femininity also preoccupies John Podhoretz in *Can She Be Stopped: Hillary Clinton Will Be the Next President of the United States Unless . . .* On the one hand, Podhoretz *wants* to like Hillary, even though he finds her tough to warm up to as a woman: she never figured out what to do with her hair and clothes, in his diagnosis, she isn't a raving beauty, and her manner is almost pathologically unsexy. Interestingly, Podhoretz, who tries to present himself as a reasonable guy (in this group the bar is set pretty low), thinks this anti-feminine quality may actually work in her favor: being "neither girlish nor womanly" with a "hard to describe style" could be the perfect blend for the first woman president, he muses, since a president has to be a little scary, not seem emotional—basically she should be an unlikable bitch. "And Hillary is a bitch." * Feigning worry that saying this kind of thing makes him sound sexist—while clearly admiring himself for saying it—he explains that a woman presidential candidate needs to show she can be manly, and if any woman politician can pass for a tough guy, it's Hillary. This scares him, though in a sweaty, enthralled sort of way. Call him Mr. Conflicted.

If Podhoretz is all over the map about Hillary, no doubt he has his reasons. As with his fellow biographers, we have reason to believe that his own intimate relations are not without their complications, especially when it comes to women and politics. For one thing he's a neocon currently married to a northern liberal, as he himself reveals in the Hillary bio. However, those who pay attention to such things may recall his previous marriage to a more like-minded Beltway conservative following a whirlwind ten-day courtship, during which Podhoretz declared his love for his new amour in his *Weekly Standard* column ("In her calm, there is the permanence I seek"). Unfortunately, the permanence proved short-lived—the relationship unraveled rather publicly after a brief three months.

But maybe inner maelstroms come with the territory when Mom is the ultra-conservative doyenne and fiery anti-feminist Midge Decter, author of numerous books denouncing the women's movement and the dupes who fell for it. And Dad is the notoriously pugnacious neocon Norman. When Podhoretz says, incoherently, that Hillary had an "easy path due in part to feminism," he sounds like the dutiful son, channeling Midge. What mother could ask for more? But things can't have been easy for John: between

---

* So firmly entrenched is this assessment among Hillary haters that when she momentarily teared up during the New Hampshire primary, this too was taken as evidence of her bitchery: she cried *strategically*.

the powerhouse mom, his own romantic impetuosities and flip-flops, and the politically strange-bedfellows current marriage (though I'm sure they're a lovely couple), Podhoretz has more than his share of family baggage when it comes to love and politics. As has Hillary herself, needless to say—in a better world the two of them could have a fascinating heart-to-heart on the subject.

Instead, Podhoretz spends a good chunk of his book proffering weird advice to Hillary on how to position herself to win the election, even while bashing her senseless at every turn. Example: to avoid being upstaged by Bill, Hillary should treat him "as though he were her *father*—there to provide her with emotional support and little else." Here we pause to note that Podhoretz is someone whose career has always been upstaged by *his* more famous father. How can the reader keep her footing amidst this mad swirl of relatives, husbands, ambitions, and projections?

By the way, R. Emmett Tyrrell has some free advice for Hillary too: she should get herself a divorce, and pronto. Since Bill is not only goatish but also "ithyphallic" (I had to look that up too), Hillary could present herself to women voters as "a victim of the male penile imperative," then start dating again. I imagine Tyrrell is so pro-divorce because his own life improved so dramatically following one, especially on the penile imperative front. His fans will doubtless recall Tyrrell's bubbly reports about life as a swinging bachelor, picking up "terrific co-eds" at various right-wing think-tank shindigs, and not returning home alone. Yes, conservatives do score, as Tyrrell—who charges Hillary with having been too self-disclosing in her memoir *Living History*—makes sure to let us know. His preference is for the "soignée" and "physiologically well-appointed," though unfortunately one of his soignée dates is mistaken for a hooker when he drops by a conservative gathering at the Lehrman Institute on his way to Au

Club, a then-happening Manhattan nightspot. (A friend explains to Tyrrell that when a conservative shows up somewhere with a beautiful woman, he's usually paying by the hour.)

Tyrrell has actually been quite the gallant about aging female Republicans in the past, waxing lyrical about right-wing sex kitten Phyllis Schlafly's foxiness and Nancy Reagan's large beautiful eyes, both of whom are perhaps a quarter century his senior—to which one can only say, "You go, Bob."

But could he ever go for a Democrat? As most agree, Hillary's aging well, and Tyrrell hasn't been *entirely* critical. On the plus side, she reminds him of Madame Mao, the "white boned demon" who was never more dangerous than when wearing a seductive guise, and Tyrrell is on record as a man who likes a seductive guise. However, in an exceedingly strange passage toward the end of the book, we learn that Hillary's ultimate dream is to be commandant of a "national Cambodian re-education camp for anyone caught wearing an Adam Smith necktie or scarf." Or perhaps it's also an extermination camp, since he adds: "Welcome to Camp Hillary. Please remove your glasses and deposit them on the heap. (Was that a flash of gold I saw in your teeth?)" Yes, it's off to the killing fields for Tyrrell and his kind—having received her political education at the feet of Pol Pot, it's definitely curtains for the bourgeois enemy once Hillary takes the reins. I think Tyrrell means all this to be witty. He concludes by telling readers he's "taking the high road, since hatred is an acid on the soul."

Here we've entered the realm of male hysteria, where reason and intellect go to die, though Tyrrell can be a hoot for those who find this kind of thing entertaining.

Speaking of male hysteria brings us to the peculiar case of Tyrrell's protégé at the *American Spectator*, David Brock, and his biography *The Seduction of Hillary Rodham*. Except in this case the acorn *does* fall far from the tree. After Brook received a million-dollar book advance to write a smear job on Hillary similar to the one he'd previously performed on Clarence Thomas accuser Anita Hill (Brock was famously the author of the "a bit nutty and a bit slutty" line about Hill), a strange thing happened when he tried to plunge the dagger again. Somehow he couldn't. Sure there was the stuff about the sixties radicalism that Hillary never really abandoned, including a catty analysis of her college wardrobe. And like the rest, he spends countless pages enumerating her bodily crimes and misdemeanors: given her thick legs, she adopted the sort of "loose-fitting, flowing pants favored by the Viet Cong" (just call her Ho Chi Rodham); along with these, she sported white socks and sandals (here, even I must protest), wore no makeup, piled her hair on top of her head, and "came from the 'look-like-shit school of feminism.' " Even once ensconced in the professional world, she cut a "comic figure" with her hair fried into an Orphan Annie perm and a "huge eyebrow across her forehead that looked like a giant cater-pillar."

But more of the time it's an intermittently compassionate por-trait of a gawky, brainy, well-intentioned midwestern girl swept off her feet by a charismatic southern charmer who migrated to the backwaters of Arkansas—or Dogpatch, as Brock likes to call it—to advance Bill's political fortunes, sacrificing herself and her principles for love. Bill repaid her by having sex with everyone in sight. But Hillary wasn't a phony, and shouldn't have had to play the part to advance Bill's career, Brock insists—he even says that her physical appearance should never have become a political issue, notwithstanding the amount of time he devotes to cata-loguing it.

One of the fascinating aspects of Brock's employment situation was that he happens to be gay and the *Spectator* happens to regularly fulminate against gay rights, as did his yappy boss Tyrrell whenever given the chance. When Brock speculates that Hillary might have been "perversely drawn to the rejection implied by Bill's philandering," willing to accept compromises and humiliation in the sexual arena because of the greater good she and Bill could together accomplish, Brock—who'd once thrown a gala party to celebrate the hundredth day of Newt Gingrich's anti-gay Contract with America—could have been describing his own career arc too. The big problem for him was that he ended up identifying with Hillary when he was supposed to be vilifying her, and it turned his life upside down. Some mysterious alchemy took place in the course of his writing this book: instead of exposing Hillary to the world, she exposed Brock to himself. The result was a stormy breakup with his pals on the Right: he became persona non grata in his former circles, or maybe he dropped them first.

But he and Hillary had some sort of imaginary bond, at least in Brock's imagination. He describes waiting in line for several hours at a bookstore for Hillary to sign his copy of *It Takes a Village*, and where he hoped to stage their first face-to-face meeting. The question on his mind, he confesses, is *what she thinks of him*. No doubt it's the private question every biographer entertains at some point about his subject. But when he reaches the head of the line, faces up to the real Hillary rather than the imaginary one, identifies himself and asks when he could have an interview, Hillary's wry reply is "Probably never."*

. . .

---

* Not only did they eventually meet again, but Brock went on to become a major Clinton fund-raiser and self-styled media advisor; he recently started an opposition research shop called Correct the Record to aid her 2016 campaign.

"All biography is ultimately fiction," Bernard Malamud wrote in *Dubin's Lives*, his novel about a biographer. What would he have said about this particular collection of writers: all biography is ultimately a Rorschach test? The various Hillaries that emerge are fictive enough, yet clearly they have some inner truth for their creators. Each invents his own personal Hillary—from baroque sexual fantasies straight out of *The Honeymoon Killers* and girl–girl sexcapades, to big sis—then has to slay his creation, while paying tribute to her power with these displays of antagonism and ambivalence. They're caught in her grip, but they don't know why; they spin tales about her treachery and perversity, as if that explains it. Except that the harder they try to knock her off her perch, the more shrill and unmanned they seem.

A clue comes our way from Dorothy Dinnerstein, who wrote some years ago in *The Mermaid and the Minotaur* of the "human malaise" in our current sexual arrangements—namely, the arrangement where men rule the world and women rule over childhood, and mothers are the "first despots" in our lives. To her haters, Hillary is nothing if not a would-be despot making an illegitimate grab for power. She wants to run the world!

Now, I'd never say that men who hate Hillary are treating her like a bad mother, since it would sound like a huge cliché. But according to Dinnerstein, the psychological origin of misogyny is simply the need for mother-raised humans to overthrow the residues of early female dominion. Or to put it another way, men aren't going to give up ruling the world until women stop ruling over childhood, meaning that if political power is ever really going to be reapportioned between the sexes, child rearing would have to be reapportioned too. For the most part, this has yet to happen, meaning that it's not hard to see why the prospect of women ruling *both* spheres, a woman with her finger on the button of world destruction *and* in command of the home, prompts such massive anxiety.

Power isn't a geopolitical matter alone. It inheres in the very experience of being ruled—and that's what being a citizen means. But we were also all children once, who got pushed around by big despots with their own agendas for us. Too often it can seem like adulthood is just one long reprise, with a slightly larger cast of characters. As to how this plays out in terms of political psychology—well, that's what's being renegotiated at the moment, in a predictably bumpy way.

Or *is* it really something about Hillary in particular? It's hard to deny that for this collection of men, the very sight of her, ankles to hair, just puts them in a dither. What female colossus is this they're all flailing at, what oversized mythic figure? She's monstrous, Gorgon-like; not feminine enough, *or*, conversely, deploying feminine wiles to further her nefarious ambitions. She's their Medusa—who had her own hairstyle issues, let's recall. Her snakelike hair made men stiff with terror—turned them to stone, as Freud aptly put it in an essay about male anxiety. So stiff, in fact, that images of Medusa's decapitated head were often emblazoned on Greek shields as a reassuring emblem for soldiers going to war.

If only Hillary could have the same salutary effect on today's embattled men! Or maybe that's the point of these slashing biographical portraits—cut her down to size and stiffen your own . . . resolve? What's clear is that the specter of loss looms large for these men of the Right: a woman has run (and will probably run again) for president, and the small matter of who's in charge of the world and how power is divided between the sexes is up for grabs.

. . .

As speculation about the 2016 lineup builds, commentators on both sides continue to focus below the belt for portents. One of the narratives currently being floated is that disappointment in Obama's performance as president helps reposition Hillary on the gender spectrum, or as Democratic strategist James Carville recently remarked, "If Hillary Clinton gave Obama one of her balls, he'd have two." This was pretty provocative—and intended to be, obviously, on all sorts of levels.

The relation between the sexual organs we've been assigned and what happens to us in the world as a consequence is fruit for a constantly evolving orchard of metaphors. Though of course what happens to us in the world isn't metaphorical: it's simply the case that fewer positions of power go to the humans with the vaginas than the humans with the penises.

At the end of the day, whether you have one or the other thing going on down there hasn't yet stopped mattering. There may be a small number of people who've traded in the sex organ they were born with, and a small number who are otherwise ambiguously situated (and have their own battles to contend with because of it), but generally it's been a binary universe we're born into and mostly still is. Even as gender has supposedly become more mobile, even as there are all sorts of exciting new roles available on either side of the divide—women senators, male nurses and strippers—what's evident from reading Hillary's biographers is that we're nowhere close to giving up the idea that what's down there is the key to everything.

But if Carville's metaphorical reassignment of genital equipment means that, going forward, whenever someone says that someone else has "balls" we have to rethink the relation between power and manhood, because metaphorically speaking, women have balls too, then maybe the categories do start looking more arbitrary, or "fungible" as the lawyers say. And maybe the cause–effect relationship between genitals and power isn't an arrow moving one way or another anymore, but starting to look more like a Venn diagram, with lots of weird angles and unexpected possibilities.

Women Who Hate Men

Sex with men is bad for women, and I mean *bad* in every sense of the word: from the dismal quality of the experience itself, to the lasting harms it inflicts—psychological, social, and existential. At least this is a premise with a certain traction in the cultural imagination, and seems in no danger of losing its hold, even in an era that simultaneously pays frequent lip service to the polar opposite premise, that sexual parity between men and women is now an established fact, and sex is finally good for women, so let's all party. In short, there are lots of conflicting stories making the rounds about what women are getting up to in bed, and how much they're really enjoying it, and whether proclaiming enjoyment is even a reliable indicator of anything when it's a woman doing the proclaiming; we are the gender, after all, notorious for faking enjoyment. In fact, if you're a woman, even good sex may be bad for you in ways you can't begin to calculate.

The literature of bad sex is alarmingly extensive (as is bad writing about sex, though these aren't necessarily the same thing), and a mainstay of the genre is the cautionary tale aimed at dissuading women from having sex, or sex of the wrong kind, or with the wrong people. The arguments vary, the politics varies, but the message keeps coming around again, like a hit single on the Top 40 station. By far the most interesting variation on this theme is Andrea Dworkin's 1987 radical feminist classic, *Intercourse,* now repackaged in a twentieth-anniversary edition. In case you've forgotten, Dworkin was the notorious anti-pornography activist and theorist most famous for having said that all intercourse is rape, though she claimed she never actually said that.

The reprint arrives with a new introduction by Ariel Levy, the author of *Female Chauvinist Pigs.* Levy was less a fan of Dworkin's in *Pigs,* labeling her an extremist, which is undoubtedly true yet also a little backhanded, given that Levy was reprising so many of Dworkin's arguments, albeit in more measured tones. But I too must admit that I never had much use for Dworkin and have ranted against her in print on a few occasions, though rereading her this time around was strangely enjoyable. She's the great female refusenik, and just because sex disgusted her it doesn't mean she isn't often funny and even profound on the subject.

Previously I was under the impression that it was only heterosexual sex that disgusted Dworkin, but that's not the case. As Levy's introduction helpfully informs, Dworkin, who died in 2005 at the age of fifty-eight, may have proclaimed herself a lesbian but she wasn't known to have clocked any hours in the actual enterprise, either romantically or sexually. Additionally, she was an unorthodox enough lesbian to have loved and secretly married a man, her soul mate, with whom she cohabited for over three decades—he, too, was gay, and happened to have health insurance. A soul mate with health insurance and no sexual demands! Happily, Dworkin found the kind of love she either believed in or could tolerate: one that didn't involve bodies or the messy meeting up of alien genitals. She had far less confidence in the ability of other women to hew to similarly nonconformist paths, I suspect not without reason.

Dworkin was an extremist because she kept harping on the nasty undercurrent of inequality in sexual relations between men and women, and she wouldn't let it drop. In fact, she seemed to revel in it. Of course, more mild-mannered and even anti-feminist writers keep strumming this same banjo too: namely, the idea that men get more out of sex than women do, even when women think they're operating in some liberated fashion, turning the tables and having recreational sex just like the guys. Nope, they're dupes and doing irreparable harm to themselves in the process. The difference is that for Dworkin, intercourse isn't a personal thing or a private folly; it's a form of political occupation equal to what all colonized peoples have endured over the centuries. At least this meant she refrained from dispensing chirpy advice on how to get more foreplay, or land a man by playing hard to get, or other quick fixes to female dilemmas. Dworkin didn't believe in individual solutions, and she didn't think a little freedom was enough: she wanted to overthrow the whole fucking system.

This seems unlikely to happen anytime soon, but Dworkin is still an excellent philosopher of the bedroom, if a fumingly vitriolic one. Even if you disagree with everything she says, she's great exactly because her work resists all practicality. *Intercourse* is a furiously unreasonable book, and usefully dangerous for just that reason: it forces us to look at sex without trying to *solve* it.

Dworkin's premise is startling and will always be radical: in short, that sexual intercourse itself is what keeps women mired in a state of social inequality, because a "normal fuck" is an act of incursion. Perhaps a few of you female readers previously thought of sexual intercourse as a "natural" act; maybe even thought you liked it. Dworkin will have none of this. Sex, along with the desire for it, is forced on women to subordinate us. During intercourse

a man inhabits a woman, physically covering her and over-
whelming her and at the same time penetrating her; and this
physical relation to her—over her and inside her—is his possession of her. He has her—or, when he's done, he has had her. . . .
His thrusting into her is taken to be her capitulation to him as
a conqueror; it is a physical surrender of herself to him; he
occupies and rules her, expresses his elemental dominance over
her, by his possession of her in the fuck.

Note the passive construction—"is taken to be"—a hallmark
of the Dworkin style. Elsewhere: "The normal fuck by a normal
man is taken to be an act of invasion and ownership undertaken
in a mode of predation." Taken . . . by whom? The passive voice
combined with the punch-you-in-the-face argument, the vacilla-
tion between victimization and militancy: this is Dworkin distilled to her essence.

Dworkin was a grandiose writer who liked playing with omniscience: she wanted to speak from within the dark tangled un-
consciousness of sex itself, then expose it to the interrogator's
rubber hose. Not just expose it, she wanted to hold a war-crimes
tribunal—*Intercourse* is her one-woman Nuremberg trial on the
injustices of heterosexual sex. Indeed, she was fond of comparing
intercourse—along with its propaganda arm, pornography—to
the greatest crimes of the twentieth century: Treblinka, Ausch-
witz, the Gulag all come up as parallels. She was never one for
understatement.

Her favored prosecutorial tactic is to pick a revered literary
author and ventriloquize him: at one moment she's Tolstoy, at
another Kobo Abe, then she takes a spin as Isaac Bashevis Singer.
Characters merge into authors who merge into the singular truth
of the entire culture; writers of every era and nationality are
assembled to testify to the violent timeless truths of male sexual

hatred for women. You can read very attentively and still not be entirely sure who's speaking from one sentence to the next—Flaubert? Patriarchy? Dworkin? This is rhetorically powerful, if slippery. This is my life, she wants you to think. (Don't get defensive about it or you'll just prove her right.)

Given the slippery stylistics, Dworkin can be tough to pin down theoretically. It's never exactly clear in her account what's a cause and what's an effect: whether women are an inferior class because intercourse subordinates us or intercourse subordinates us because we're already an inferior class. But if the problem is fucking per se, then won't penetrative sex always be oppressive? Or does she just mean penetrative sex, for women, in a male-dominated society?

On this, as on much else, Dworkin is charmingly inconsistent. What's nature, what's culture—why quibble over details? At certain points we hear that women are anatomically constructed for subordination—after all, we're the ones with a hole that's "synonymous with entry," put there by the God who doesn't exist (Dworkin is a virtuoso at the droll aside). At other points we hear that male power constructs the *meaning* of intercourse, because men get off on dominance. Regardless of whether it was nature or culture that made things inequitable, it's doubtful it can ever be otherwise, at least not until everyone gives up fucking. (Dworkin is fairly indifferent to the reproductive aspects of the act, but then how much intercourse is really for reproduction anyway?)

You can find her paying very occasional lip service to the possibility of a non-male-dominated society in which a more woman-oriented sexuality would hold sway, though this turns out to be the conventional soft-focus stuff: "diffuse and tender sensuality that involves the whole body and a polymorphous tenderness." This, Dworkin assures us, is what women really want. As far as bringing about the social conditions under which tender sensuality would achieve primacy in the bedroom, it's hard to see how this is going to happen since men enjoy their dominance too much and women are too complicit in helping them maintain it, especially by getting horizontal with them all the time.

Obviously, Dworkin was not the world's biggest fan of men: not only are they titillated by inequality, they need it in order to perform at all. Men get pleasure from sexual hatred, and intercourse is their way of expressing contempt. It should be noted that Dworkin's own contempt for male sexuality runs just as deep as theirs for women: without rape, pornography, and prostitution, "the number of fucks would so significantly decrease that men might nearly be chaste." This is just one of her many indictments of the brawny sex. One is tempted to point out that Dworkin either underestimates or just never noticed the vast range of male vulnerability possible in sex. Her men are all into "cold fucking," and whether they're husbandly or promiscuous types, their "eventual abandonment turns the vagina into the wound Freud claimed it was"—one of her nicer aperçus. Just as all women really want tender sensuality, all men really want to degrade women.

Considering that Dworkin was so devoted to flattening men and women into reassuringly predictable types, it's curious that one of her main anxieties about sex was that it makes people generic. Fucking *is* the great universal event, but for her, the universality means that we lose our individuality in the very act. She seems anxious about the breakdown of boundaries that can happen in sex, even though boundary-blurring is what people frequently seem to like about sex, or so I hear. But for Dworkin, it was abhorrent, a threatening loss of self, because in intercourse "nothing is one's own, nothing, certainly not oneself, because the imagination is atrophied, like some limb, dead and hanging useless, and the dull repetition of programmed sexual fantasy has replaced it."

Maybe the best way to read Dworkin is as the literary writer she aspired to be rather than as a social theorist. She said her models were Dante and Rimbaud, though the contemporary writer she brings to mind is novelist Michel Houellebecq—her acid eloquence on the subject of empty sex matches his; her hatred of men matches his disdain for everyone, apparent in the way he sets his characters banging into one another in mutual incomprehension and loathing. No one is better than Houellebecq on the general repellence of human physicality, but Dworkin gives him a run for his money. For both, the contemporary mantra that sex is good for us is the emptiest notion of all, the new patriotism. Dworkin: "We talk about it all the time to say how much we like it—nearly as much, one might infer, as jogging." Ouch. "This is the sexuality of those who risk nothing because they have nothing inside to risk." Ouch again. Dworkin may have been the great hater of sex, but is she wrong when she charges that the bubbly "sex-positivity" of our time masks a deep and abiding core of disgust?

Dworkin's own writing teems with sexual disgust, but it's disgust that transforms itself into flurries of creative loathing and poetic incantations. Out of the vast woman-hatred of the culture, she created a seductively sordid idiom:

> There are dirty names for every female part of her body and for every way of touching her. There are dirty words, dirty laughs, dirty noises, dirty jokes, dirty movies, and dirty things to do to her in the dark. Fucking her is the dirtiest, though it may not be as dirty as she herself is. Her genitals are dirty in the literal meaning: stink and blood and urine and mucous and slime. . . . Where she is not explicitly maligned she is magnificently condescended to.

It's hard to argue. Any woman who won't admit it just enforces Dworkin's view that we lose any capacity for self-knowledge and honesty in sex, since to the extent we reconcile ourselves to enjoy-ing it, our brains turn to mush. Worse, women transform them-selves into pathetic sex scavengers, wanting sensuality and tenderness but settling instead for "being owned and being fucked" as a substitute for the physical affection and approval we actually crave from men. Women need male approval to be able to survive inside our own skins, and solicit it through sex; but obtaining sex means conforming in "body type and behavior" to what men like. Given the vast amount of time, energy, and dis-posable income many of us invest in achieving and maintaining whatever degree of sexual attractiveness is feasible (sometimes known as "fuckability"), again, it's hard to argue. Self-knowledge might be the means to really *knowing* a lover in sex—the only thing that makes passion personal instead of generic—but self-knowledge is impossible for women because having intercourse in the first place requires eroticizing powerlessness and self-annihilation. If the argument seems tautological, you're getting the point: fucking is a vortex, an abyss, a sinkhole from which you never emerge.

The topic that Dworkin is not entirely persuasive on, no sur-prise, is pleasure, which is pretty much absent here except as a form of false consciousness. (She's far more animated by vio-lence.) For a woman, trying to eke any portion of pleasure out of sex is collaborationism; initiating sex is taking the initiative in your own degradation. There's no entry for pleasure in the index, though you'll find entries for "Sex act: repugnance toward" and "Sex act: used to express hatred." You must wait until page 158 to find orgasms even mentioned in the text—or more accurately, lack of orgasms, since here she's citing Shere Hite's data to the effect that seven out of ten women don't experience orgasms from intercourse. Dworkin seems not unpleased. How *could* a woman have orgasms under such conditions, she wants to know, in which we have to turn ourselves into things because men can't fuck equals? Who'd enjoy this kind of thing but colluders and dupes?

Yes, Dworkin reads like a stampeding dinosaur in our era of bouncy pro-sex post-feminism. Feminist anger isn't exactly in fashion at the moment: these days, women just direct their anger inward, or carp at individual men, typically their hapless husbands and boyfriends. Nevertheless, the theme that sex injures women more than men continues to percolate through the culture, though in a well-meaning nibbled-to-death-by-ducks sort of way, in books with titles like *Unhooked: How Young Women Pursue Sex, Delay Love and Lose at Both* or *Girls Gone Mild: Young Women Reclaim Self-Respect and Find It's Not Bad to Be Good*. The arm-twisting subtitles tell you everything you need to know. The general worry is that casual hookups have replaced dating, young women are having too much sex, and girls who are slutting around are never going to find husbands. Besides which, it's supposed to be woman's task to train men to act better than they do, and this is no way to go about it. Also, with so many women hooking up with no strings attached, things aren't fair for the girls who won't. Not hooking up these days sounds like trying to unionize in a right-to-work state—if everyone else is selling it cheaper, how's a higher-priced girl going to stay in the market?

It's all very alarming, but the new alarmism is so *tepid* compared with the old alarmism. Dworkin had her female fears, obviously, but for her the problem started with female anatomy, not being a bad girl: "Women are unspeakably vulnerable in intercourse because of the nature of the act—entry, penetration, occupation." Her successors can't follow her down this path— they're equally invested in female fragility, but indicting intercourse itself would implicate marital sex too, and marital sex is supposed to be the reward for virtue, in their version of the story. Dworkin saw womanhood as a tragic condition, but at least she wasn't peddling the line that everything used to be better in the old days, and the best solution is finding a man to love and marry you.

All in all, if I have to cast my vote for a sexual alarmist, I'm for Dworkin, the radical firebrand, in lieu of the well-meaning aunties. Sex for her was catastrophic and disgusting, but at least she wasn't trying to spawn a generation of nice girls. True, she had no time for sexual experimentation—she disliked men too much to admit that nice girls stifled by conventionality and greedy for freedom have always pursued it by trying to act like men, whether that means careers, adventurism (from Joan of Arc to Amelia Earhart), or sleeping around. Emulating men has its problems, to be sure—they haven't got it all figured out either, other than how not to buy books telling them to have less sex, which is probably why no one writes them. For my money, this in itself would be a condition to aspire to.

There's no doubt that women are often pretty deluded about their reasons for wanting sex with men—it's been true enough in my life, anyway. People want to—and frequently do—have sex with each other for murky and self-deceiving reasons, or for clear-eyed reasons that turn out to be mistaken, or a thousand variations on the theme of erroneous judgment. What Dworkin couldn't concede is that what pushes against your boundaries, what destabilizes—maybe even chafes—can also remind you that you're alive.

CODA

To bring things full circle, Andrea Dworkin and Larry Flynt may
not be anyone's idea of a great match, but they did have one
intriguing encounter—not in person but in the courts, naturally.
Dworkin had brought a $150 million lawsuit against Flynt and
Hustler for calling her, among other things, a "shit-squeezing
sphincter" and "one of the most foul-mouthed, abrasive man-
haters on Earth." They also said she advocated bestiality, incest,
and sex with children.

Dworkin lost. In a surprisingly ringing defense of rhetorical
excess, the Supreme Court of Wyoming compared *Hustler*'s
over-the-top language to the historical confrontation between
labor and management—a "widely recognized arena in which
bruising and brawling, rough and tumble debate is the daily
fare." The moral and political clashes between pornographers and
anti-pornographers are waged in the same heated spirit, said the
court. "Abusive epithets, exaggerated rhetoric and hysterical
hyperbole are expected."

What the decision also made clear is that someone over at

Hustler had read Dworkin very thoroughly, possibly more thoroughly than she'd read herself. It seems she *had* written favorably about bestiality, incest, and sex with children, in a chapter titled "Androgyny, Fucking and Community" in her book *Woman Hating*. Imagining a model society where sexuality as we know it would be overhauled, Dworkin envisions eliminating the incest taboo to foster the free flow of natural androgynous eroticism, human and animal relationships becoming more explicitly erotic, and children being allowed to live out their own erotic impulses. Eventually the distinctions between adults and children would completely disappear. Though Dworkin insisted she was only discussing these possibilities not advocating them, the court ruled that *Hustler* was entitled to critically interpret her work as it saw fit—criticism is "a privileged occasion," they wrote, and an inherently subjective enterprise.

There's something delicious about this all-male panel of Wyoming justices and the editors of *Hustler* poring so assiduously over Dworkin's outré fantasies about androgyny and community. Though what's poignant in retrospect is that Dworkin's prodigious capacities for overstatement and hyperbole were matched only by *Hustler*'s; Dworkin and Flynt were partners in their fondness for excess (perhaps also on the exciting dirtiness of sex). They definitely kept an eye on one another: there was a mutual fascination, enlivened by mutual abhorrence.

A similar mix of attraction and ambivalence has propelled me through these essays. I said at the outset that we're in search of our split-off other halves, but it's easy to miss them given the weird and disconcerting forms they sometimes take. The idea here was to be a crash test dummy, so to speak; open to the possibilities of accidental collisions—to the surprises and perversities, and not least, the ruptures to various articles of faith about what it is to be a man or a woman. Consider this an interim report.

ACKNOWLEDGMENTS

Most of these pieces had earlier incarnations; my thanks to the editors who helped shape the ideas and writing the first time around: "Scumbag," Joy Press (*Village Voice*); "Con Man," Chuck Kleinhans and Julia Lesage (*Jump Cut*); "Trespasser," David O'Neill (*Bookforum*); "Juicers" and "Cheaters," John Swansburg (*Slate*); "Lothario" and "Gropers," Meghan O'Rourke (*Slate*); "Victim" and "Humiliation," Michael Miller (*Bookforum*); "Critic," Ann Hulbert (*Slate*); "Hillary," Amy Grace Lloyd (*Playboy*); "Women Who Hate . . . ," Jennifer Szalai (*Harper's*).

Many thanks to Jacob Weisberg, who first enlisted me at *Slate*, which was a great stomping ground and a place to experiment with ideas. Thanks also to my agent, PJ Mark, and to Connor Guy at Metropolitan for his careful readings and attentions. To my fabulous editor, Sara Bershtel: words (and grammar) fail me, or are at least totally inadequate to convey my gratitude, which extends far beyond the stuff on the page. And thank you to Jim Livingston, for being brilliant, unstinting, and a sweetheart.

ABOUT THE AUTHOR

LAURA KIPNIS is the author of *How to Become a Scandal,* *Against Love,* and *The Female Thing,* which have been translated into fifteen languages. A professor in the Department of Radio/TV/Film at Northwestern University, she has received fellowships from the Guggenheim Foundation, the Rockefeller Foundation, and the NEA. Her writing has appeared in *The New York Times, Harper's, Slate,* and *Bookforum,* among other publications. She lives in New York and Chicago.